THIRD EYE
AWAKENING

GUIDED MEDITATION TO OPEN YOUR THIRD EYE, EXPAND MIND POWER, INTUITION, PSYCHIC AWARENESS, AND ENHANCE PSYCHIC ABILITIES

SARAH ROWLAND

Third Eye Awakening

Guided Meditation for Chakra Healing, Chakra Balancing, and Chakra Cleansing Guided Meditation Techniques to Open Your Third Eye, Expand Mind Power, Intuition, Psychic Awareness, Enhance Psychic Abilities, and much more!

Sarah Rowland

Table of Contents

INTRODUCTION

Congratulations on getting your personal copy of *Third Eye Awakening*. Thank you for doing so.

Throughout this, you will learn several things about the third eye along with other techniques that will improve your life.

In chapter one we will cover what exactly the third eye is, and what it does, as well as it's connection with the pineal gland.

In chapter two we will talk about the different ways that you can open your third eye chakra

In chapter three you will find you first meditations. These are basic and easy meditations, and you will find a third eye meditation.

In chapter four you will learn how to balance your chakras and why this is important.

In chapter five you will learn about chakra meditation.

In chapter six you will learn what mindfulness meditation is, and you will find mindfulness meditation practices.

In chapter seven you will find a chakra meditation practice that you can use to balance your chakras.

In chapter eight you will learn about your higher self and how to awaken it.

In chapter nine you will learn about your divine self and how to connect with it.

In chapter ten you will learn the importance of trusting your intuition.

In chapter 11 you will find meditations that will help you on a personal level. These are more advanced than some of the other meditations.

In chapter 12 you will find out how to clear out negative energy

In chapter 13 you will learn how you can heal yourself with only your mind.

In chapter 14 you will learn how to awaken you psychic awareness

In chapter 15 you will find several meditations that will help you to heal different areas of your life.

In chapter 16 you will learn how to clear out your energy fields

In chapter 17 your will learn the importance of positive thinking.

In chapter 18 you will find your last chapter of meditations that will help to boost your energy.

There are plenty of books on this subject on the market, thanks again for choosing this one! Every effort was made to ensure it is full of as much useful information as possible. Please enjoy!

Chapter 1: Your Third Eye

The third eye is a person's ability to see what could be, to see their potential.

Everybody can access their third eye. Yes, the third eye is invisible, but it is as available and present as the other two eyes. It is a huge source of intuitive wisdom that can get amplified by meditation. It can give us forewarnings, insight, and a high level of intelligence into our past, present, and future. The best way to open the third eye is by meditation.

The third eye chakra is found between the eyebrows. It encircles the pineal gland, lower section of the brain, head, and eyes. It is an energy field that we can use to tap into what we can't smell, hear, feel, taste, or see.

It is a spiritual chakra that means beyond wisdom. It will lead you to the knowledge that guides you if you let it. When you open this eye, it can give you a visualization, expanded imagination, lucid dreaming, telepathy, and clairvoyance. This sixth sense transcends our basic senses and makes itself known as gut feelings. Your third eye knows and sees the unseen.

We experience the world with our five senses. Before you were born, you heard noises such as outside sounds, your mother's heartbeat, and voice. You experienced taste, touch, and perceived light. Since your birth, you attribute what you experience with what you get with your senses. You learn to trust your senses in what you hear, see, touch, smell, and taste. Sense perception is great when experiencing life, but it can limit you when you want to expand your awareness.

At one point in your life, you had to depend on your inner knowing. We had to rely on the environment and primal instincts to help guide us. Like birds know when a tsunami is going to hit, or ants know when to begin gathering food for winter, humans must have intuition. We have lost touch with it and the ability to trust it.

Have you ever had a feeling like someone you care about is in trouble and have received a call to justify your feelings? Have you felt like someone is watching you and you stop and turn around to see a friend from school looking at you? Have you ever been thinking about someone and then get a call from them moments later? This is your third eye trying to lead you.

The old saying about everything you need to know is already inside you is very true. It is possible for you to develop and harness this ability.

The Third Eye is a part of everyone. It doesn't matter what your religious beliefs are or your gender, we all possess this unique and powerful third eye. Most of our third eyes haven't been activated. They remain unawakened, dormant, closed and calcified.

You don't have to have a crystal ball or tarot cards. Don't spend money on an expensive psychic to give you answers to what you seek. What you want to know is already within you and is accessible with your third eye. If you feel conflicted, as your intuition to open up to you and help you make the correct choice. When you open up this dimension, prepare yourself for a more thoughtful, intelligent, meaningful, conscious life before you.

With every new meditation session, it will shift your consciousness to a higher state. It will release your worries and anxiety from every moment of your life. This means forever.

Your stressful concerns about how you will be able to pay your credit card bills, student loans, or mortgages will soon just evaporate. It will be replaced with present, and clear thoughts about how you can be successful and the premeditative version is laughable. With your third eye activated and opened, everything becomes crystal clear, and you will see how to fulfill it.

Meditation allows you to become more self-aware. You will be able to control your emotions and easily handle your stress. Meditation tunes you into intuitive wisdom.

Many cultures consider intuition the most important sight or sense we possess. They have practiced third eye meditation for centuries.

Someone new to meditation has reported feeling a tingling sensation around the third eye area or feeling a slight headache. If you get a pulsating or tingling around the third eye either after or during meditation is a signal that this once blocked chakra is opening.

While you are meditating, learn to become more aware of how much inner intelligence you possess. You will need to continue to open and activate your third eye to its full capacity.

Health issues? Your third eye can help you fix the problem. Relationship problems? Your third eye can attract people to you. Financial or career problems? Your third eye knows the process to success. Figuring out and fulfilling your life's purpose? Your third eye knows what you need to choose at every moment in your life.

Think about how your life could be if your infinite inner wisdom could be accessible when you need it. Meditation is the best solution.

All of us are human, and we all strive to have a life free of fear, but we worry about how we are going to do our daily tasks. This only creates more worry. Like attracts like and this is extremely true with thoughts.

Most all successful people owe their fortunes and fame to trusting what they received from their third eye.

If we can set a time aside every day to meditate, we can change how our thought takes root. We start to have fewer negative thoughts, anxieties, and worries. When they disappear, what is going to take their place? A strong, in tune, the omnipresent law of attraction.

As your third eye begins to open, your emotional, mental, and physical health will improve and multiply. Higher and new level souls will start to enter your life, and this will result in better relationships.

Your third eye will make the right path to success as clear as your hand in front of your face. Meditation can help you manifest abundance as easily as you breathe.

If you want to know what is out there for you, but you are not sure what it is, there is no need to fear. Any questions you might have about your life like your job, relationship, or achieving your dreams can be answered from the information that you receive while meditating.

When you activate your third eye, meditation will allow you to see and understand the sound and sights of the world that was once hidden. It allows you to optimize your present life with the vast new information. Be an observer of the unseen. Make what was once impossible for you are possible. Meditation will unlock your infinite potential.

You can think of the third eye as an organ that contains your mind and every one of your senses working as a large, powerful sensory organ. It is a clever evolution that will allow you to see patterns within your life. What's more amazing is that your third eye reveals patterns by overlaying information on top of the other senses.

You can use your third eye as a sense in various ways. Seers use theirs to understand connections and answer hidden questions. Energy workers can feel the energy around them, and they manipulate the energy. Each time you have empathy, you use your third eye to feel and touch other's emotions.

To better understand how the third eye works, let's find out how to use your third eye to interpret and sense the energy around you. You can see motion (a car moving), activity (you are driving the car), and the exchange of energy (car burning the gas). Add in the ability to sense and project the potential (predict where the car will go by basing it on roads and the driver). You can see where the energy, motion, and the activities will go with time. Add this to a visual map, and you have just seen energy playing out. Being able to see the energy as an overlay instead of just a concept, it will become a property of life that will help us learn how to interact and sense deeper.

Can you see energy? No. We can see the end results of energy but seeing energy is different. We can only see what our eyes are designed to see and that is light. Our third eye processes information and overlays that information over the other senses in a way that can be interacted and interpreted with energy to be more precise. By doing this, we understand where energy is and allow us to see it.

If you take the time to think about it, it does make sense. The mind already knows something and is trying to tell us. The best way it can do this is by using out other five senses.

This might appear as a power to predict or see certain events that are not present physically. It is a tangible and extremely real skill.

Third Eye Awakening

It all depends on the ability to interpret the results. There is plenty of room to mistranslate what are facts and what the third eye tells you. Since all of us see things differently, it could be a problem to share this ability with others. If you hear the word cat, everybody will visualize a different cat. What one person sees is different from others. Each person's unique nature makes sure we all see the world differently.

It is not surprising that there are a lot of mystical practices for everyone to explore all the perception in the world.

If you think about a person who can see auras, these are just another sense overlay. Your brain can process visual information, but what it creates for you is limited to what you see with your eyes. Think about a page as you read it. It is just lines. You are seeing words and the concepts and ideas that are laying on top of that.

Think about another person. You aren't just seeing what they are wearing. Your complete network, your sense organs, and mind create a larger antenna that can pick up patterns and energy in front of you. There are many clues that can tell you about this person's level of distraction, well-being, and emotional state and many other things. Your third eye puts this information in what you are seeing by giving them an aura. What you see is different than what is happening. Your mind alters your experience to give you more information to work with. The third eye uses our mental capacity to alter the perception and add in more data.

Seeing auras is looked at as a mystical power and depends on the person's skill level. But it is a tangible skill and one that can be taught. You can be taught to see auras in the standard way.

Taoist practices have an extensive training practice for working and using your third eye. It is a meta sense and must be tuned and used to be developed fully. It's not something that works straight out of the box after birth.

Many will suppress their ability to keep others from making fun of them or calling them crazy. With a lot of suppression, this ability will go away. You have to use your third eye for it to work. How you use it will shape what you can sense. For these reasons, the third eye continues to be a mysterious ability.

Each culture will use different techniques to mold this skill. Taoists are patient and take decades to refine this ability in order to become a Seer. The nature of this ability means that experience can help you improve its accuracy and capabilities. It is a slow process to master.

There is a wonderful breathing technique called the bee breath. This is done by bringing both hands up to your face. Put your two middle fingers over the eyes. Have the index fingers resting on the eyebrows and the pinky under the cheekbones. Stop up your ears with the thumbs. Inhale a deep breath and exhale with the word AUM. Have the emphasis on the M and create a buzzing sound just like a bee. Continue this for two minutes or longer. This can alleviate tension that is in your heart and it can help to open the third eye.

If you are into yoga, any pose where the forehead is pressed down will help the third eye. Try dolphin pose it is helpful when you lift your head to look at the floor. Child's pose is another good one where your forehead is pressed to the floor or yoga block.

The color of this sixth chakra is indigo. The mantra is SHAM.

Gems that will help to open the third eye are azurite, lapis lazuli, and amethyst.

Chapter 2: Opening The Third Eye

Most people want to feel better. Some want to experience a connection to another realm that might exist. You must have the balance to be able to maintain these high frequencies.

Everything has a vibration or frequency. The higher the frequency, the more it is vibrating, and it will be more difficult for us to see it with our physical eyes.

If you want to heighten your intuition, you want to tune it to the frequencies, so you will be able to sense the metaphysical energies.

This higher wisdom and intuition can come alive when the energy center is opened and balanced. For some of us, developing the abilities of the third eye might seem out of reach.

Here are some steps that can help:

Cultivate Silence

Nurture the silence of your mind, either with meditation, sitting calmly, or get absorbed in your favorite activity.

Why do you need to do this? Because the third eye elevates the senses to a level, some like to call in between. This space houses your psychic abilities and the realm of the invisible. It gives you the ability to listen to the information that comes through the third eye. You need to be ready to perceive its whisper. If your mind is noisy, you won't be able to hear its message.

Hone Your Intuition

There are different ways to foster your intuition. The third eye houses your higher wisdom, vision, and insight. You can get acquainted with the meanings of your dreams. Maybe give lucid dreaming a try. Learn how to read tarot cards or a horoscope. Find new ways to bring it into your daily life.

You can look at it this way, fake it till you make it. Just learn to be curious and learn about the techniques. These practices will become more familiar, and you will get more confident with your abilities with time.

Don't take this seriously. Have fun, explore and keep your chakras and mind open to the wonder and possibility.

Nurture Your Creativity

Let your imagination run free by focusing on certain activities and letting your creativity flow. Start by learning a new craft or art. Let your inspiration go through your hands. Be prepared for the surprising results. Don't worry about being perfect.

Creativity is a great way to loosen up your rational mind. All that mental chatter that makes a comment with everything you do. It doesn't matter if it is wrong or right. It will try to control every action with an intended outcome.

If you can calm that part of your brain that wants to be in control, you can focus your creativity to open other possibilities. Your third eye will have more capacity to blossom and unfold.

Ground Yourself to Soar Better

It may not be obvious that we need to have both feet firmly on the ground to open the abilities of our third eye. You also need to open it up gradually. First, build reliable foundations to allow yourself to be able to properly interpret your perceptions with clarity.

We need to have energy running through our entire energetic system and body to support the opening of healthy channels of perception. Once the third eye is activated, the information that starts coming through may seem disturbing, unfamiliar, or unusual to your mind.

Having plenty of energy and being grounded will allow us to expand into the perception dimension. It will help us open and stay away from the negative symptoms of the opening of the third eye like feeling confused or disoriented.

Now that the third eye is open let's cover some ways you can support the opening of your third eye.

Here are some practices that will give your intuitive energy center a boost:

- The main function of the third eye is intuition. You need to exercise this.

- The light of the moon resembles the light in your intuitive center so rest under the light of the moon and reflect.

- Learn to be silent and hear the wisdom of your third eye. Learn to listen. The third eye's voice is a whisper.

- Strengthen the third eye and your throat chakra's energy. They are both anchors to unlock the energy of the third eye in balanced and powerful ways.

- Practice divination.

- Lucid dreaming, dream interpretation, dream work.

- Practice visualizing.

- Silent and guided meditation.

- Let your imagination soar.

- Focus and see the in-between space things.

- Have curiosity about the meanings of symbols that are around you from different times and cultures.

- Be one with the energy and nature of the elements.

- Have fun making creative things like crafts.

- Free flow.

- Work with spirit guides and inner guidance.

- Practice meditation.

- Enrich your psychic abilities.

Be free to explore and enjoy the exploration. This is the best way to get the energy going into the third eye.

An open and balanced third eye will support intuition, focus, and concentration. Here are some techniques to help balance its energy:

Breathe

Mindful breathing can help to calm the mind and open and cleanse the third eye. Breathing doesn't just cleanse but can balance the chakra system, too.

Add Color

The third eye is associated with the color indigo. Indigo is a combination of deep blue and violet. Bring purple and blue into office and home décor. Surround yourself with a subtle tone that can help to heal the sixth chakra and boost your energy. Add semi-precious or precious purple or blue jewelry to your accessories.

Practice meditation

The exercises that require you to engage the third eye are the best. Meditating and visualizing the color purple or blue can activate the sixth chakra.

Concentrating on these colors won't just open the energy center, the bit will help heal and balance the chakra.

Dream

The third eye is critical in dream recall and dreaming. Activate and engage your third eye by writing in a dream journal.

Work the theta brainwaves

Third Eye Awakening

It is useful to learn how to maintain and activate the alpha and theta brainwaves. These support the frontal lobe activity and help to prepare the brain and third eye to be receptive.

Add fragrance

Bring essential oils into your body, bath, and home. Fragrances work great to balance, cleanse, and open the chakras. To activate and heal the sixth chakra, try one or more of these oils:

- Nutmeg
- Grapefruit
- German or Roman chamomile
- Myrrh
- Sandalwood

Drink or eat vegetables and fruits

Eating foods and beverages with natural purple and blue colors can boost positive energy going through the third eye. Drink dark juices like blackberry and grape. Add the following vegetables and fruits to your grocery list:

- Beets
- Rainbow chard
- Prunes
- Eggplant

- Blackberries
- Blueberries
- Black currants

Yoga

When you start learning how to heal and open the energy centers of your body, there isn't a conversation complete without talking about yoga. The practice includes elements of movement, focus, and breathing and when done together are great for balancing and cleansing the chakras.

To strengthen and open the third eye, try these yoga poses:

- Salamba Sarvangasana or Supported Shoulder Stand
- Adho Mukha Svanasana or Downward-Facing Dog
- Balasana or Child's Pose
- Ardha Uttanasana or Standing Half Forward Bend
- Virasana or Hero

If you want to heighten your intuition don't fall into these traps:

Give up Easily

You don't expect to become a master carpenter overnight so don't expect to be able to see auras or angels after your first meditation. You don't want to wake up and be standing face-to-face with the ghost of your Grandmother. In the early stages, this will probably scare the bejesus out of you.

If your goal is to feel metaphysical energies, get ready to take a beautiful journey to self-discovery. Take as much time as you need to adjust to the frequencies and let those old habits go that are keeping you at a lower frequency. It is a beautiful process so enjoy it.

Hold on to Old Habits

Look around you. Do you see angels? If you don't, there probably aren't any, and that is because you have a block that is keeping you from being able to see them. That block is acting like a blindfold. This block can't take your intuition away. It just hides it temporarily.

Some common blocks are stuck emotions from your past, a harmful home or work environment, a diet full of chemicals, a toxic relationship.

If you want to heighten your intuition, it will be necessary to take inventory and figure out what is hindering your perception and then let it go.

Taking in Too Much Energy

If you have empathy, you pick up energies from others within your environment. You start to feel energies around you plus your emotions and thoughts. The gets exhausting very quickly. If you find yourself in this position, you have to get yourself grounded.

Children have great spiritual energy. They are pure lights in the world. What do they do? They jump, skip, hop, run, move, and play. The need to move as much as adults need to move.

When you push your body while playing sports, swimming, jogging, hiking, you are changing your physiology. When your feet hit the ground, the sweat, the moves are a recipe that helps you release all the negativity and ground the energy that is making you foggy.

If you don't get grounded, you could find yourself trying to ground by other activities like reading, watching TV, scrolling through negative media, engaging in conflict, or eating. These are not ways to ground yourself.

To be able to feel better and get rooted in your body and the moment, move your body. Do it every day for two weeks and see if you feel better.

Third Eye Awakening

Getting Lost in the Realms

There is a harmful way to meditate. There are many spiritual seekers who seek spirituality as a way to escape everyday life.

Your spirit guides, angels, and soul is already here. The goal is to be aware of them and not get lost in their world. It is easier than you might think. Some people treat meditation like drugs, alcohol, or playing video games. They live there and use the language where they talk about aliens, councils, realms, and things that don't have any practical value in our lives.

If you meditate just to find a world to escape to, you will find such a place. If you look for information, you will find it. If you look for scary energies that threaten life here, you will find these energies.

You need to seek being that wants to help you to make your life a wonderful reality. Remember you are only here for a reason. You don't live on another planet or in another reality. You belong here. We don't know for how long. So, make the most out of this one. Use your perception to add color and flavor so you can enjoy and enhance your reality instead of leaving it behind.

Chapter 3: Basic Meditation

In this chapter, you will find a few basic meditation practices. These are perfect for a person that is new at meditation, or if you only have a few minutes to spare. These are all short meditations that will never take more than ten minutes of your time. Let's begin.

Two Minutes to Calm

Begin by taking a deep, cleansing breath, and once you're comfortable, close your eyes.

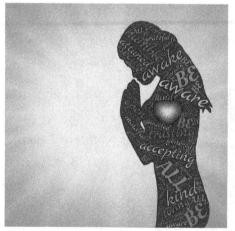

Take a moment to imagine yourself feeling more focused, calm, and peaceful. As your unconscious mind starts to create this calm image of how you would feel; think of what you may see, hear, and how you may feel that tells you you're more focused, calm, and peaceful.

At this point, you may already be feeling more focused, calm, and peaceful. If you're not feeling this way, notice what you're unconscious mind is telling you to do so that you can feel that way.

Now think of how you can use this image in your life to help you feel calm in the days and weeks ahead. Once you have figured this out, remember that it is that easy to create calmer and peace in your life.

Take another deep, cleansing breath, and start to bring your attention back to the present moment. Listen to the noises in the room and slowly open your eyes.

Now ask yourself, what did you learn?

Three Minute Mindfulness Meditation

Select a comfortable, upright position, either on the floor or a chair. This should be a position that you can stay in for three minutes. You don't want you back, legs or bottom to start hurting. This distraction will interrupt your practice.

Once you're comfortable, set a timer for only three minutes.

Begin by thinking about a mental anchor. This could be anything. You could think about movements or sensations within your body, how your breath feels as it travels through your nose, ambient noises, count numbers, or a mental image that you find relaxing or comfortable. This can be anything that can anchor your attention to the moment. Invite this into your mind and let it be.

As you sit and think about your anchor, other thoughts will start to creep up. This is normal. When the mind wanders, bring yourself back to your anchor. Continue this until your three-minute timer ends.

Three Minute Breath

Begin by sitting in a comfortable position, take a deep breath, and notice how your feet feel against the floor. Take note of every sensation in your feet.

Lay your hand on your belly and take two to three deep breaths and notice how your stomach rises and falls with each inhale and exhale. Once you are relaxed and comfortable, close your eyes.

As you continue your deep belly breaths, start breathing in for a count of five, hold that breath for another count of five, and then release the breath for a count of five. Continue this breathing pattern, breath in for five, hold for five, and release for five, for one minute.

Now begin to bring your attention back to the present slowly. Notice the sounds in the room, and slowly open your eyes.

Five Minute Relaxation

Get settled into a comfortable seated position. As you take a deep breath, relax your feet flat on the floor and notice how they feel. Take a few more deep breaths and center yourself at the moment.

Bring your focus to your toes. Scrunch up all of your toes, and then release them. Move your attention to your ankles and allow them to relax. Move up to your calves; tense and release them. Next tense and relax the muscles in your knees. Move onto your thigh muscles, tense and relax.

Allow any thoughts that may come up to float away from you like tiny bubbles.

Now move onto your buttocks; tense and release the tension. Now release the tension in your pelvic area. Now start to notice the tension that you may have built up on your back. Slowly take a deep breath in, and as you release the breath, slowly *allow the tension in your back to release.*

Move your attention onto your shoulders. Pull your shoulders up towards your ears and then release them completely. Great, now move your attention to your neck and jaw muscles. Slowly take a deep breath, and as you release the breath, all the tension in this area to release.

Lastly, move to the top of your head. Bring your shoulders towards your ears again and then release them, now any tension that is remaining in your body will sink and release.

Great, take a couple of deep breaths and enjoy the relaxed sensation in your body, and allow yourself to feel calm. Sit like this for a minute.

Once you're ready, start to bring your attention back to your surroundings. Notice the sounds around and slowly open your eyes.

Fifteen Minute Third Eye Meditation

Start by getting in a comfortable seated position. It's best to sit cross-legged on the floor. If this is uncomfortable for you, try sitting upright in a chair with your back straight and your shoulders relaxed. You can also do this laying flat on the floor, but there is a risk of you going to sleep.

Once comfortable, take a deep, long breath in through your nose, and as you exhale, take your attention to the middle of your forehead, between your brows and slightly above the brow line. Imagine that there is an indigo-blue chakra sitting there. The dark glow of this indigo light begins to illuminate your mind and then spreads out through the rest of your body.

Create a door to your mind with your third eye. Imagine yourself opening this new door and walking through it into an empty room. Take a moment to decorate this room however you would like. Pick colors, looks, and décor that makes you feel calm and happy.

Make sure your room suits your tastes perfectly so that this area is now your new personal sanctuary.

Locate an area of the room that is the most comfortable and takes a seat.

From this position take a look out onto the world. Bring into your mind that same ideas, situations, issues, and thoughts that plague your everyday life. Take a few moments to contemplate these things silently.

Now image your sixth chakra spinning and gaining strength. The fast it spins, its indigo light washes over your body and invades all of your cells, and every pore of your body.

Take a deep breath in and feel all the energy bursting out your third eye as rays of dazzling indigo light.

Rest in this sensation for a few moments.

Still, in your mind, stand up for your peaceful place and walk back to the door you created earlier. Walk out of the room and look back into your new

sanctuary and notice how you feel one with it.

Once you are ready, bring your attention back to the present and slowly open your eyes.

Chapter 4: How to Balance Your Chakras

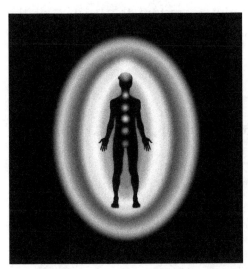

When people talk about balancing their chakras, they might be referring to different meanings and techniques. An accepted definition of chakra balancing is the process where the chakra's energy is brought into a harmonious and functioning state.

Balancing your chakra is just a part of the picture: Every chakra is a part of the system that works as a whole. We can see that each chakra has a connection with the other and they interact energetically. When we balance our chakras, we have to think about each chakra, their neighbor, and the energy they hold as a whole.

Balancing your chakra falls into three categories. The ones centered on physical activity or process, an introspective or meditative practice, and the passing of energy from another or on your own.

- Some common practices that you can use to balance the chakras are:
- Alternative or holistic medicine.
- Breathing practices like pranayama.

- Exercises that focus on connecting the mind and body, this includes yoga.
- Self-inquiry and meditation.
- Energy or hand on healing.

There are some practices that aim to restore the balance of the chakras for well-being. The common ones are:

- Pranic healing
- Craniosacral therapy
- Reiki

Using healing crystals or stones can support chakra balancing activities.

Why do you need to balance your chakras? To support a flow that sustains your overall energy level. We are subjected to many activities that are sources of demands and stress that causes fluctuation in our energy. Some might feel draining, fulfilling, or nourishing. Past experiences and events can leave an influence on how we feel in the world and therefore influences how we manage our daily energy.

Stress that is placed on us by life's demands might result in fluctuations and interruptions in our flow of energy and imbalances in our chakras. Chakra imbalances could cause:

- How energy flows through the chakra or chakra system.
- The energy to become closed-up or blocked.
- The energy flow to increase excessively and isn't regulated.
- The chakra's energetic field get displaced.

Balancing regulates energy when it is too much, establishes a consistent flow when there isn't enough, and aligns where there is a displacement.

The seven main energy centers than run through the body are called your chakras. Each one is situated at a different location, so they each correlate with different dysfunctions and ailments. Each energy center houses our emotional and mental strengths. If we have a physical issue, it can create weakness in our emotional behavior. When we get rid of that bad energy, it can relieve any malfunction, stiffness or tightness in that area.

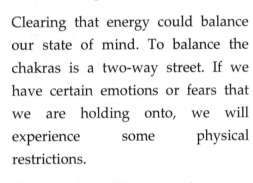

Clearing that energy could balance our state of mind. To balance the chakras is a two-way street. If we have certain emotions or fears that we are holding onto, we will experience some physical restrictions.

If you have stiffness or achiness or some recurring fears and emotions, read on to find out what chakra might be blocked or affected.

Using affirmations is very effective in balancing our chakras. Thoughts are able to create your reality. When you start regularly using chakra balancing affirmation, you will achieve amazing results.

Chakra translates to a spinning wheel. Each chakra corresponds to a certain color-coded vibration within the universe that influences our spiritual, emotional, and physical well-being. If the chakras are aligned perfectly with the universal energy, each aspect of our lives will be joyful ad harmonious. We can claim perfect health. Our passion and love for live will be renewed.

When you use the affirmation, lie or sit in a comfortable and quiet place where you can focus. When speaking an affirmation, picture a wheel spinning in a clockwise direction in the color that is specific to every chakra.

The Root or First Chakra

This chakra sits at your tailbone on the base of your spine.

Imbalances in the root chakra can cause physical problems with the prostate gland, male reproductive system, immune system, tailbone, rectum, feet, and legs. People who have imbalances in these parts are more likely to experience problems like constipation, eating disorders, sciatica, knee pain, and degenerative arthritis.

Imbalances can also cause emotional problems like the feelings that affect our survival needs like food, shelter, and money and the ability to provide for what we need in life.

If this chakra is in the balance, you will feel grounded. You will have a sense of safety and connection to this physical world. You will feel supported.

This chakra provides the lesson of self-preservation. Everyone has the right to be here.

The root chakra relates to the color red.

To help get this chakra back in balance, say this affirmation: "I am a being of light. I am secure, protected, and peaceful.

The Sacral or Second Chakra

This chakra is found two inches below your belly button.

Imbalances can include physical problems like low back, pelvic, and hip pain, kidney dysfunctions, urinary problems, reproductive and sexual issues.

Imbalances in your emotional problems can include being able to commit to relationships. The ability to express emotions. The ability to have fun or play that is based on sexuality, pleasure, creativity, and desires. Fears about addictions, betrayal, and impotence.

If this chakra is in the balance, we will be able to take risks. We will be committed. We will be creative. We are outgoing, sexual, and passionate.

This chakra teaches the lesson of honoring others.

The color that relates to this chakra is deep orange.

To help get this chakra back in balance, say this affirmation: "I am strong, beautiful, and radiant. I enjoy a passionate and healthy life."

The Solar Plexus or Third Chakra

This chakra is located three inches above your belly button.

Imbalances in the solar plexus chakra can include physical problems like colon diseases, gallbladder and pancreas issues, stomach ulcers, diabetes, high blood pressure, chronic fatigue, liver dysfunction, and digestive problems.

Imbalances can include emotional problems like our inner critic emerges, self-esteem, and personal power. We will have fears of making physical appearances, getting criticized, and being rejected.

If this chakra is balanced, we will have self-compassion and self-respect. We will feel like we are confident, assertive, and in control.

This chakra teaches us self-acceptance.

The color for this chakra is bright yellow.

To get this chakra back in balance, say this affirmation: "I am successful and positively empowered in everything I do."

The Heart or Fourth Chakra

This chakra is located at your heart.

Imbalances in the heart chakra can include physical problems like wrist and arm pain, shoulder and upper back problems, issues with the lymphatic system and breasts, lung disease, heart disease, and asthma.

Imbalances in this chakra can cause emotional problems like

bitterness, anger, abandonment, jealousy, over-loving to causing suffocation, issues with the heart. You might have a fear of being lonely.

If this chakra is balanced, you will feel compassion, love, gratitude, and joy. You will forgive easily and learn to trust.

This chakra teaches us to love.

The color of the heart chakra is a vibrant green. Just think spring.

To help rebalance this chakra, say the affirmation: "The answer to everything is love. I receive and give love unconditionally and effortlessly."

The Throat or Fifth Chakra

This chakra is found at the throat.

Imbalances with the throat chakra can cause physical problems like shoulder and neck pain, problems with the tongue, lips, cheek, and chin, ulcers, ear infections, TMJ, laryngitis, sore throats, and thyroid issues.

Imbalances can cause emotional problems like expressing oneself with written or spoken communication. Being fearful of not having any choice or power. Not being in control or having no willpower.

If this chakra is balanced, there will be free communication, expressions, and words. We will be truthful and honest but firm. We will be great listeners.

This chakra teaches us to speak and lets the voice be heard.

The throat chakra relates to a pale blue color.

help rebalance this chakra, say: "I express myself clearly and truthfully. My thoughts will always be positive."

Third Eye or Sixth Chakra

This chakra is found in the middle of the forehead right between the eyebrows.

Imbalances can cause physical problems like hormone function, hearing loss, seizures, eyestrain, sinus issues, blurred vision, and headaches.

Imbalances can cause emotional problems like self-reflection, volatility, moodiness. You won't be able to look at your fears or to learn anything from others. You will daydream often and be in a world that has an exaggerated imagination.

If this chakra is balanced, we will feel focused and clear. We know the difference in illusion and truth. We will openly receive insight and wisdom.

This chakra teaches us to see the bigger picture.

The third eye chakra relates to the color dark blue.

To rebalance this chakra, say this affirmation: "I understand the meaning of all life's situations, and I can tune into the divine wisdom."

Crown or Seventh Chakra

This chakra is located on the top of the head.

Imbalances can cause physical problems like sensitivity to the environment, sound, light, problems learning, and depression.

Third Eye Awakening

Imbalances can cause emotional problems like great power and self-knowledge. The imbalances can come from thoughts about spirituality and religion. Being constantly confused. Being prejudiced. You might have a fear of being alienated.

If this chakra is in the balance, we will live in the moment. We will have great trust without inner guidance.

The crown chakra teaches us to live mindfully.

This chakra relates to the color violet.

To help rebalance this chakra, say this affirmation: "I am one with divine energy. I am complete."

You might feel that you have one or more chakras out of balance or blocked. This happens when one chakra becomes blocked, and the others are trying to compensate and become overactive or underactive.

The best way to balance the chakra is to start with the root chakra and go up to the crown chakra.

Chakra affirmation creates revolutions within our healing journey. There is nothing more effective or transformative than using your thought power to bring changes to your soul, mind, and body.

Chapter 5: What is Chakra Meditation

Just like there are seven notes in the western scale, seven ages of man, seven levels of consciousness, seven colors of the rainbow, there are seven chakras in the body. There are chakras outside of the body that helps us to connect to the universal field. These energy centers, gates, and transformers that connect the lines of the meridian with the three auras that surround the physical bodies. These are found along the spine and at the head. They can be balanced and activated with meditation.

The seven chakras sense the range of frequencies that enter the person's energy field. They distribute and process the energy that enters the auras and meridians. They transform the frequencies into various sensations like physical, thought, and emotion. This is done just like eyes refract light. Just like different light frequencies enter the brain get interpreted as various colors, the seven chakras, break down impressions that impact and radiate within a person.

The seven chakras are organs of transformation. They move the energy down or up as it comes into the body from different sources into the energy system depending on what emotional, mental, or physical area is in deficit. The chakras balance energy as it enters the energy system. This occurs with spiritual healing. Excessive energy from mental and emotional bodies are given to the physical body to heal itself.

Transfiguration moves in four different directions: out, in, down, and up. The seventh chakra is a gate that transforms the energy down from the spiritual plane into a person's energy field. The body's physical energy is transformed upward to be used in the higher parts of the body. Energy from other fields can be transformed as it goes through the person's aura and enters a certain chakra.

A person can project rays of energy out from their chakra to another person's energy. It then gets transformed either down or up depending on the energy's vibration. This usually happens with specific meditation.

The entire body is a reflection of what we believe, our emotions and thoughts. It is the manifestation of our beliefs about who we are.

We initially dream a dream about our lives, and we continue down this path of awakening to the truth of who we are. At some point, we leave this path.

Everything we experience is a representation of what we believe is true about ourselves. Most of these beliefs are in our unconscious mind.

The chakras are like energetic motors in the physical, emotional, and mental energy fields that we don't look at as a part of us. Every chakra center relates to a different area.

The health of these chakras is governed by what we believe is true in a certain area of our lives that the chakra relates to.

The root chakra relates to how we connect to other people and our survival instincts. If someone feels unsafe, then trust will be difficult. This chakra will cause us to pull into ourselves and not join in with the others.

Chakra meditation is different depending on the person and the time. Chakras might appear in different ways. What gets highlighted are places that have separation, numbness, cloudiness, density, or constriction. They may feel like they are pulling back from the other chakras. They won't feel like they are moving. They might feel like they are trying to protect itself.

Try to sense which chakra is struggling and notice what area of the body it's in. This can help you be aware of the beliefs that are related to a certain chakra.

The chakra colors are the same colors and in the same order as a rainbow. With red being at the base and violet being at the crown. We are walking rainbows. If you hold a crystal in sunlight, it will display beautiful rainbows.

We have been told that when we get upset, it is due to something happening that caused us to be upset. This is the opposite. When a bad event occurs like disease, discomfort, or pain within your body or another event like losing a relationship or job, this occurrence reflects the upset we feel within us. This is under what a person can see with conscious awareness.

As an example here, pretend that your husband comes to you and tells you he is moving out until things get better. This makes you feel horrible. This event causes a part of you to separate from another part of you. How your experience the way others treat us is the reflection of the way you treat yourself. This is how you unconsciously believe you should be treated

Your chakras will reflect this, too. Usually in the heart or solar plexus. It can affect the first two and the throat chakras, too. The cells and organs in these parts of the body are related to the chakras that rule them.

There are a corresponding body sensation and emotion that is tied to the separation. A chakra meditation is needed to simply allow this sensation and give it permission to be here.

When you are able to stay with that sensation, the associated chakra that needs healing will begin to heal and open by itself. The chakra will clear automatically.

Our bodies have the power to heal itself. You just have to allow it to happen.

With chakra meditation, if we can embrace whatever arises, the trauma inside the chakra will begin to release. This is done by letting is work and spin along with the other chakras. This will bring along balance and harmony as your energy field shifts to make a unified whole. When your energy field becomes aligned, healing will begin automatically. Our inner knowing can take care of our emotions, body, and mind when we can learn to turn towards conflicts instead of running away.

There are two different ways to approach chakra clearing, healing, and balancing. The first one covers focusing on the cause of the imbalance.

If we don't address the cause, feeling distressed and upset will persist in our emotions, mind, and body.

What is causing all the suffering and distress?

Suffering is caused by assuming we're separate instead of whole.

Compare this to a wave in the sea that is trying to locate water. It doesn't realize that it is water and one with the whole ocean it appears in. If it continues identifying itself as being a separate wave, it is going to suffer.

 Identifying that we are able to create our own belief system. If we continue to believe we're separate , we will believe that we are incomplete and inadequate. In turn, our beliefs control our

bodies, emotions, and thoughts. They will also make a whole movie about our experiences.

If we can start to experience that we are pure awareness, our lives, experiences, emotions, thoughts, and beliefs will begin to show the peace that we know we are.

To have a chakra meditation that will help your chakras to balance and heal, you have to use a meditation the helps you to bring attention to yourself. Imagine and focus on your current light, and then release everything that is standing in the way of your wellbeing and love.

You don't have an inside or an outside, you are only pure awareness that doesn't belong to a single location, and you will work with everything that is outside on the inside.

Chakra meditation that focuses different effects levels. As we become accustomed to ourselves as being pure awareness, you can use different chakra mediation variations to help ease the problems that were caused by identifying as being separate and isolated instead of the whole we are.

Use visuals and music that help to relax and calm your nervous system.

To ease the side effects of beliefs that are painful, you can use some variation of light that you could incorporate like:

- White Diamond Light that aligns and purifies energy fields.
- Green Emerald Flame that transforms and restores your physical body.
- Violet Flame which combineds gold of Christ Consciousness, the Divine Feminine rose pink, and the sapphire blue of the Divine Masculine. These colors come together to form the pure violet flame that helps to release painful memory attachments
- Pink Rose Light will infuse your being with love from the Divine Mother and makes a protection shield around and in you. This is perfect if you are in need of inner child protection and healing
- Yellow Sunshine Ray arises in our awareness as our feminine and masculine polarities become balanced and are associated with Christ Consciousness. This ray has both Divine Wisdom and Illumination.
- Gold Light is slightly darker than Sunshine Yellow. It will bring you true peace. This energy healer helps to nurture and stabilize energy fields. This is what you call after you have finished energy work to bring light in and complete and balance yourself.

You can also experiment with different variations of these while you meditate and find the ones that speak to you. Your intuition might bring other colors to you. You might find that you are drawn to a different light during different times.

As you begin resting with your pure awareness and turn loose of past trauma and beliefs, follow your inner guidance and check out healing modes you have been drawn to. There are lots of therapies out there that can help you to ease painful beliefs that appear within your mind, emotions, and body. Your inner guidance will help to show you what model is best for you

Chinese Medicine, acupuncture, and yoga are helpful because these

approach healings as a whole, unlike western medicine that treats parts and not the whole.

As you start meditation healing, you must know that you are opening your awareness that can increase awareness of unconscious materials that have been dormant just under the surface for possibly many lifetimes.

You might notice some uncomfortable sensations and feelings. This is you being aware of the energy that is growing, and not the energy itself.

Healing goes slowly. You have residue that releases layer by layer.

You aren't going to have to dig around to find them. Just notice anything that that is bothering your daily life, and that will provide you with what your need to heal. This gives you an opportunity window.

While you continue on with your chakra meditation, your healing will continue to unfold in divine timing

While you are continuing to dream this dream, the healing process will continue with each layer, as we awake fully into realizing the pure awareness that we are.

Chapter 6: Mindfulness Meditation

Another important type of meditation is mindfulness meditation. Mindfulness is the practice of bringing your attention to what is happening at the present moment, which you develop this ability through practice and meditation.

In Buddhist traditions, it is believed that mindfulness will bring you to spiritual enlightenment and end your suffering.

Many studies have been done about mindfulness, and they have found that it will help you to live a better, happier life. When you spend your life worrying, and ruminating over things that you either can't change, or are yet to come, you are living your life in negative, and this can lead to anxiety, depression, and other mental illnesses.

When you first start practicing mindfulness meditation, start with ten minutes a day for your first few sessions. Once you have become used to the practice, increase the amount of time by five or ten increments, whichever you think you can do successfully. The goal is to get to 30 minutes a day. You can practice for longer if you want, but it isn't necessary.

The goal of mindfulness if teach you how to live in the moment. While you may think you already do, stop and think about where your mind is when you're living. When you eat your breakfast, do you taste your food appreciate  what it is doing for your body? Probably not. With mindfulness, you will learn how to have your mind and body doing the same thing.

The best place to learn about mindfulness is within the Buddhist tradition. We get the term mindfulness from the Pali work sati and the Sanskrit work smrti. Smrti means "to bear in mind," "to remember," or "to recollect." Sati's meaning is also "to remember."

Now that you understand what mindfulness is let's move onto a few meditations to help you get started living mindfully.

Three Minute Body and Sound

Start by taking notice of your posture at this moment. You could be lying down, standing, or sitting. Notice how your body feels as it is at this moment. Now see if you can notice the sensations that are currently present in your body at this moment in time.

You may notice a lightness or heaviness, weight or pressure. You may even notice coolness, warmth, movement, pulsating, or vibration. You can notice these sensations anywhere throughout your body. The only thing you have to do is notice them.

Notice these things with interest and curiosity. Take a deep breath in. As you breathe in, allow your body to relax. Don't do anything other than be present and aware of your body.

Now allow all of those sensations to release. Now turn your focus to the sounds around. These can be inside or outside of your room. There could be many different types of sounds. Quiet sounds, or loud sounds. You should also take notice of the silence that happens between the sounds. Notice how the sound come and go.

The mind has a tendency to want to concentrate on those sounds. It starts to come up with a story for the sound. Or you think you have to react to it: I don't like that, I like that.

Instead, see if you can only listen. Take notice of it with interest and curiosity. The sounds are just coming and going.

Now turn your focus again to your body; presently standing, lying, or seated. Take note of obvious body sensations. Take another deep breath. Allow your body to soften. Once you are ready, slowly open your eyes.

Nine Minute Loving Meditation

To start this meditation, allow yourself to feel relaxed and comfortable where you are seated. In this practice, you will cultivate positive emotions, particularly, loving kindness. Which means your desire someone to be happy, or for yourself to feel happy.

This isn't dependent on anything, and it's not conditional. This is only allowing your heart to open to yourself or someone else. Take this moment to check in with yourself to see how you feel right now. Allow whatever is here, to be here.

Allow your mind to think of something. This should include someone, as soon as you think of them, you feel happy. See if you can bring someone to mind. This could be a friend or a relative. It's best if it's somebody that you have a non-complicated relationship with. It should just be a general sense, which once they come to mind you feel happy. You can even choose a child.

If you are having a hard time of thinking of a person, you can also choose a pet. Any creature that is easy to feel love for. Allow them to come to mind.

Feel as if they are standing in front of you. You can see, feel, and sense them. As you picture this, take note of how you feel inside. You could feel the warmth, or your face may feel warm. You could also start smiling or have a sense of expansiveness. This is a loving kindness.

This feeling is natural, and everybody can access it at any given moment. Now that you have this loved one if front of you, start wishing them well. Wish them to be protected from danger, and to be safe. Wish them to be peaceful, and happy. Wish them to be strong and healthy. Wish them to have well-being, and ease. You can wish them exactly what I said, or you can use your words.

Notice the sense of allowing this loving kindness come from you, and how you are begin touched by your loved one.

During this, you may have images come to mind, notice light or color, or you could have a feeling. The words you say to you loved one can bring more of these feelings. Say whatever is most meaningful to yours. Wish them to be free of anxiety, stress, and fear.

While you are sending them these words and feelings of loving kindness, check with yourself to see how you feel. Picture your loved one has turned around and has started to send these feelings back to you. See if you can receive this loving kindness from them and take it in.

They're wishing you well, to be happy. This means you. Wish you to be at ease and peace. Wish you to be protected and safe from all danger. Wish you to have wellbeing and joy.

Allow yourself to take this in. If you have not started to feel this loving kindness, or you never have in other meditations, it's not a big deal. This practice is to plant seeds. If you start feeling something other than this loving kindness, check into that feeling. What is it that you're feeling? You may need to learn from this feeling.

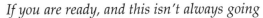

If you are ready, and this isn't always going to be easy, but try to send yourself some loving kindness. You can picture this as a light flowing down your body from the heart. All you need is a sense of it. Say to yourself; I wish to be protected and safe from danger. I wish to be strong and healthy. I wish to be peaceful and happy. I wish to

accept myself for who I am.

Then, when you ask yourself, "what will make me happy?" notice what comes up, and offer yourself that. I wish to have meaningful work, close family, and friends, a joyful life.

Now check in again and notice how you are feeling. Now think of one person, or group of people, that you want to send loving kindness to; picture them sitting or standing in front of you. Sense and feel them.

Wish them to be peaceful and happy. Wish them to be free of all fear, anxiety, and stress. Worry, grief. Wish them to have happiness and joy. Wellbeing.

Allow this loving kindness to expand outward. Allow it to spread and touch everybody that you want this feeling to touch at this moment; in every

direction. This can be people you do or don't know. People you have problems with. People who you love unconditionally. Imagine this feeling touching and expanding, and every animal or person it touches is filled with loving kindness. Every person is changed.

You can picture that everybody, everywhere is peaceful and happy and at ease. Once you're ready, take a deep breath in, and open your eyes.

Chapter 7: Chakra Meditation

We've covered the importance of chakra balancing to help improve your life, and this chapter will provide you with meditation that will help you balance your chakra. While the other meditation chapters have multiple meditations, this one will only have the one. This is because this one meditation covers all of your chakras. Make sure you set aside enough time to go through this meditation. This meditation will take about 25 minutes, and is not ideal for you very first meditation.

It's important that you have experience with basic and mindfulness meditation before you begin this chakra meditation. Let's begin.

Sit in a comfortable position, either sitting cross-legged on the floor, or in a chair with your back straight. Let your eyes close and lower down into your breathing, relax your belly, and soften your mind.

Notice and feel how you are supported and connect with the ground below. Allow your weight to sink into the floor, chair, or cushion.

Notice all the sounds around you, and allow them just to be. Take note of the shade and light, and the air is touching your body.

Sense how the sky is above you, the horizon is stretched out around you, and the earth below you, supporting your weight.

Let your mind release and empty out everything that doesn't need to hold onto. Allow it to leave, flow out, and away. Let your body do the same thing. Let it release everything that it doesn't need hold onto. Allow it to leave; flow through you, and away.

Take yourself away from the things that you have been through in your day. Bring all your energy to your center and ground yourself in the present moment. Start to notice the area around you. Breathe along with space, and notice the rise and fall of every breath. Notice how it's coming and going, its sensation, temperature, and sound.

Breathe down into the area where your body weight rests, below your spine, into your root Chakra. Breathe into this area. Allow it soften and grow with your breath, bring nourishment and life force energy into it.

Let the root connect into the ground below you, deep within the earth. Bring in the color red, the color of earth. Allow your root to be bathed in red: grounding, embodying, empowering you the present moment. Allow your root to take everything it so desires. Speak these words: "I am here," "I have every right to be at this moment, as I am," "The earth will support me."

Once you are ready, continue up to your belly, just below the bellybutton, to your Hara, emotional intelligence, pleasure, movement, creativity, and

choice chakra.

Move your breath into your Hara. Allow this area to soften gently and expand with your breath, bring in life force energy and nourishment. Invite in the color orange, the setting sun's color. Allow your Hara to be bathed in the color orange: motivating, empowering, and balancing. Allow your Hara to be fed and say: "I honor all my needs," "I will allow myself nourishment."

Once you feel ready, move your focus on the soft area just below the breastbone, your Solar Plexus, your power chakra.

Breathe into this area, letting the solar plexus to expand and soften gently along with your breath. Invite the color yellow in, the color of the sun. Allow your solar plexus to be bathed in the sunshine: nurturing, restoring, and replenishing. Allow the solar plexus to take everything it needs. Say the following: "I am worth my weight in gold," "I am enough," "I am more than enough," "I greatly value myself."

Once you are ready, move up to the center of the chest, the heart, unconditional love and self-development chakra.

Breathe slowly into your heart, allowing it to expand and soften with your breath. Allow in the color green, a spring color, or the color rose pink, whichever speaks to you. Allow your heart to be bathed with healing, renewal, and nourishment. Allow your heart to take in all it desires and speak, "I am nourished with love," "I will give and receive love freely," "I am completely loved."

Once you are comfortable and ready, move onto your neck, the throat, personal will and self-expression chakra.

Let the throat to expand, soften, and breathe. Invite in the color blue, the skies color. Allow your breath to be the sky into your throat, freeing creativity and self-expression, softening control needs, opening, and clearing. Allow the throat to take in what it needs. Say, "I will go with life's flow" "I express myself" "I speak and hear the truth."

Once you are ready, move your focus up to the forehead, between the eyebrows, the third eye, the intuition and wisdom chakra. Allow it to breathe, expand, and soften gently.

Invite in the color indigo, the color of the night sky. Allow your third eye to be bathed in indigo; understanding, insight, clarity, balancing, and soothing. Allow the third eye to take all it desires. Say; "Everything is unfolding as it should."

In your own time, move your focus to the top of the head, your crown, the oneness chakra. Allow your crown chakra to breathe.

Bring in the color violet and softly bathe your crown chakra in the violet; harmonizing, restoring, and balancing. Allow your crown to take everything it needs. Say, "I am one with the whole" "I am one with the universe."

Once you feel ready, bring yourself back to the whole, back into the normal flow of the breath, back into your center. Breathe deeply into the core, and say "I am perfect as I am" "I am whole."

Let the words energy to bather you spirit, emotions, mind, and body. Allow your body to take everything it needs. In your time, allow yourself to become aware of the air touching your body. Then notice all the sounds near you and far away.

Let your chakras close a little, all you need is the intention. Notice the support you have below. Take note of how it feels now and hold you in loving kindness, for the amazing, unique, and beautiful person you are. Once you feel ready, bring you a meditation to a close and slowly open your eyes and notice how you feel and how your surroundings have seemed to change.

This meditation should not be used an everyday practice. Use this only when you feel like you chakras need to be cleaned. You can also set a schedule for when you use this meditation, once a month, with the change of the seasons, or any other schedule that works best for you.

Chapter 8: Awakening Your Higher Self

In 1923 Dr. Sigmund Freud wrote an analytical paper about the Id and the Ego. From this perspective, the ego was created to be a survival mechanism. The super-ego is your spirit. As you awaken this understanding, your Spirit is carrying out your plans.

This is sometimes called your higher self. Your Spirit carries the gifts of intuition, claircognizance, clairsentience, clairaudience, and clairvoyance. Stored in your DNA is the multi-dimensional part that never left the garden. Your subconscious is the way to it.

The mind only processes forty bits of info each second. The subconscious is a million times more powerful. The subconscious mind stores the past, but it lives in the present. This mind will replay in your mind the events that took place in the past. The ego trusts no one, expects the worst, never forgets, doesn't forgive, whines justifies, judges, defends, blames, and rants.

The higher self can gain entry into your energy field. This point is an arm's length above your head. You engage your higher self by sending gratitude from the heart to that entry point.

Third Eye Awakening

The first step to connecting the higher self is quieting the ego. This is

the lower self that lives in your subconscious. If we can clear all the energies that we don't need from our subconscious, we will be able to connect to this higher self and reunite with our Spirit.

The higher self is a part of you that connects you to the spiritual realm. It transcends our consciousness. It is infinitely wise and eternal. It stays in touch with the Divine since it is a part of it. Gaining knowledge of the higher self and all its wisdom is the goal of the spirit in all its different disguises.

Every one of us connects to the Divine. The higher self-transcends all understanding of the conscious mind. This is the power that all teachers and geniuses have accessed. It is the place of miracles and magic that is in our lives.

Here are some steps to contact it:

Expectation and Belief

You must first believe that you have a higher self to communicate with. Then you need to expect that every day this communication will improve as you focus on inner growth. Without these two essential necessities, it will be hard to achieve anything in life. These two qualities are necessary for inner growth. Set a goal to make contact with your higher self, review it daily, and maintain this purpose with determination until you get success.

Transform your World View

We are raised in a materialistic world that neglects the Spirit. To establish a close connection with the spiritual realm, you must have the whole being agreeable with the goal. In all major goals, you need to make rules as to how the game will be played. Contacting the higher self is exactly the same. Find teachers and writings that can expand how you understand the universe as a fundamental being of the conscious mind.

Third Eye Awakening

Solitude

Take time to be completely alone. Make sure it is a quiet place. Sit quietly without any expectations. Do absolutely nothing. This might feel strange or uncomfortable at first. Keep going. Take the time for the inner voice to be heard. It will do it during the quiet time or sometime during the day. An event will happen, someone will give you the information you need, or you might get an insight. All the wonderful geniuses in history found time for regular silence and solitude. You need to, too.

Meditation

With meditation, you will work to discipline the inner chatter and silence the mind. You make a clean vessel that the higher self will fill. Follow your breath is a great meditation discipline since it concentrates on a candle flame. Visualize a gold ball in your solar plexus that will fill your entire body with healing and energy. There are many different practices that you can use.

Journal

Keep your insights, dreams, emotions, and feelings in a journal daily. This will get you closer to your inner intuition. You can ask your higher self-questions and then record what answers you receive. If you do this with expectations, you will receive answers.

Inner Dialogue

Have regular talks with your higher self. For 40 days, decide to stay in contact through the day. Tell your higher self that you know that it's there and you are going to pay attention to it. Ask it to speak to you and guide you. This dialogue might be one-way at first.

Remember you have not been in touch for a long time. It will take the time to clear out the cobwebs. Continue to talk just like you are talking to friends, share your hopes, ask questions, and just chat. Don't forget to listen for answers. You will get them.

Life Lessons

Look at life as a mystery. Believe that your entire life has been

constructed to teach you what you must know now. Approach life like it was created to do good for you. When something happens whether it be good or bad, ask yourself what lesson you learned. Unpleasant situations and people have been put there as a challenge. When you can view life as a drama where you play the main role, the higher self will become evident in your life. Write the finding in the journal.

Chapter 9: Astral Travel

The very idea that humans can exit their bodies while sleeping is ancient. Countless people believe it is possible to communicate with cosmic beings by vivid dreams and visions that are experienced by astral travel.

Between eight and twenty percent of people say they have had something similar to an out of body experience at one point in their lives. A sensation that their consciousness, or spirit is leaving their body. Many experience this during sleep or while hypnotized; some can do it while just relaxing.

The astral plane is one in the fifth dimension. This is where dreams take place. Where mystical teachings are given and where the dead go. You might get lucky enough to meet spiritual beings there. You can discover what happens when you die, your purpose in life, receive guidance, have premonitions about your future, have an awakening, learn wisdom about death, learn your inner defects, see your spiritual obstacles, learn what you don't know about yourself, and discover secret knowledge. You will find yourself in another world that exists outside this world. You can fly, walk through objects and walls, meet new people and travel to distant lands. It is a wonderful experience.

The reality is made by thoughts projecting consciousness into the physical realm. When you astral project, the conscious mind will leave the physical body and move into the astral body for the experience. You stay attached to your physical self through a silver cord. Some might see this cord when they astral project. To be able to astral project, you must feel completely relaxed, wear comfortable clothing, and be lying down. Put a comforter over you since the physical body might get cold when your spirit travels out of it.

You will stay aware of everything you experienced when you were not in your physical body.

Some people can do this naturally, while others are a little afraid to remove their consciousness from the physical body, so they choose not to learn.

Astral travel can be achieved either awake or through deep meditation or lucid dreaming. People who have experienced astral projection say their spirit left their physical body and moved into the spirit world. This concept dates back to ancient China, and has been around for thousands of years.

Psychics say the mind that dreams holds the astral body and this causes sudden jerks that wake you up or falling dreams. Many dreams aren't remembered and thus causes astral travel to be a

subject of individuality. Those who believe in astral travel will often mention that ghost sightings are typically described as transparent apparitions that walk along the earth.

It isn't clear if every object has an astral counterpart of if the spirit just incarnates into a body and this results in the astral travel. The phenomena might be something entirely different. Astral travel deals a little about life and the things that happen after death.

There are two different thoughts on the nature of astral travel. A broad definition of these would be a phasing model and mystical model.

The Phasing Model believes that it's possible to leave your body. The astral plane and the physical world are both areas of our conscious spectrum. When someone chooses to project, they are phasing into a different area of consciousness and the locations there. You can compare this to changing the radio station. This viewpoint is seen as the external reality is only a state that is created internally.

The Mystical Mode has many astral maps and belief systems, but are connected to the beliefs that Astral travel happens outside the physical body. An energy body is thought to carry the consciousness out of the physical body. Higher planes are reached by progressive projections of subtle energy bodies from other projected bodies. This body is connected to the physical one through an energetic connection that looks like a silver cord some refer to as an umbilical cord.

There are hundreds possibly thousands of techniques to help you astral travel. Everybody is different, so something works for one may not work for another. Try one and if it doesn't work for you, move to a different one.

The Rope Technique

The main object in this technique is to picture a rope hanging off the ceiling. The point of this rope is to provide pressure at a certain area on the astral body so that it will separate itself from your physical one

Reach out with your imagined hands and pull on yourself. Pull yourself hand over hand up the rope that is above you. You may experience dizziness. This sensation will become

stronger the farther up the rope you go.

Continue to climb and you will start to feel the vibration. Your entire body will feel like it is vibrating and you may end up feeling paralyzed. Focus complete on the climb and don not stop.

This is where you feel yourself being freed from your body. Your astral body will leave the physical in the rope's direction. You will now notice that you are hovering above your body. Now your free.

Watch Yourself Sleep

Lie down and make sure you're comfortable on your back, look towards the ceiling. Completely relax and allow your mind to let go of unwanted thoughts.

Let yourself know that you are going to watch yourself fall asleep. You will have to be clear about your intents. Let the body sleep while your mind stays alerted. Tell yourself to keep consciousness while your body is going into a trance.

Once you completely relax, you will need to become familiar with the sensations that your body has as you fall asleep. You need to be aware while this happens. You will feel your body feels numb and heavy.

Pay attention to your body's sensations. You might feel like you are floating or swaying. You might feel tingling sensations in certain areas. You could even feel vibrations surging through your entire body. You may even have buzzing in your ears. Whatever you feel, don't panic as these are signals that you are on the right path.

You need to visualize you are rising from your bed and float to the ceiling. How will it feel if you did float? Make this experience as real as you can. Hold this image. If everything works, you will notice that you are floating above your body.

The Monroe Technique

An important part of this is that you completely relax.

Now try to get yourself to go to sleep without falling asleep. Keep an awareness of being between awake and asleep. This is what they refer to as a hypnagogic state. Let this state deepen and release all of you bad thoughts. Now peer through your eyelids into the blackness.

Now relax deeper. Bring vibrations into your body and make them become more intense. You need to continue to control and grow these more. During this time is when the astral body will leace your physical body. Then roll yourself over, and you will see the physical body below you.

Out of Body Experiences from Lucid Dreams

Lucid dreams are where the dreamer is aware of dreaming. In the lucid dream, the person is already outside their body.

To achieve astral travel from lucid dreams, you need to become obsessed with out of body experiences, and you have to desire it. It's important that you read as much about it as you can. You need to think about it constantly.

When your mind is ridden with thoughts of out of body experiences, you need affirmations and triggers so you can have lucid dreams. All day long think about having a lucid dream. Ask yourself if you are dreaming now.

Third Eye Awakening

With some practice, you will be able to program your subconscious to make a lucid dream possible.

Once you're in one of these dreams, and you aware of it, you will notice that you are no longer in your body. You will be able to make yourself to see your bedroom. When you do this, your dream world will disappear, and you will find yourself floating about your body.

Displaced Awareness Technique

Shut your eyes and let yourself enter a trance state. Notice your room. Feel yourself about your shoulders and see all around. Don't acknowledge anything directly.

Now picture the astral body rotating. When you have finished the mental rotation, your astral head will be where your physical feet are. The astral feet should be where the physical head is  positioned. Now that you have this, picture the room from this perspectice.

Let go of where you are located and get rid of your sense of direction. When this is done correctly, you will feel dizzy. This is what you want

When you're comfortable, imagine floating toward the ceiling. Make this feel as real as you can. During this you will suddenly find that you have left your physical body.

The Jump Technique

When this technique is performed correctly, you will awaken from your dreams, and they will become lucid. This has to be done well.

Ask yourself repeatedly throughout the day if you're dreaming or not. It is important to do this because you need to know where you are. You have to make yourself doubt that you are in the physical world. For proof, jump just like you are flying. If you are really in your physical body, your feet will hit the ground. If you're in a dream when you jump, you will begin to float

After a few days of this, you will notice that you start to jump in your dreams to see whether or not you are dreaming. When you jump, you will be floating.

The Stretch out Technique

Lay down, close your eyes, and relax. Imagine your feet stretching and getting longer by an inch or so. When you have this in your mind, let your feet shrink back to normal. Repeat with the head. Now

alternate between your feet and head until they stretch about two feet. Now stretch them together. This starts the vibrations and will cause you to feel dizzy.

After you have practiced this a little, you will feel like you are floating and can command yourself to rise to the ceiling.

The Hammock Technique

Imagine that you are stretched out on a white hammock connected between palm trees at the beach. Picture yourself moving with the wind. Try to recreate this sensation while you picture yourself swaying back and forth. Continue this until you feel the vibrations begin to grow. Once the vibrations start, let you astral body roll out of the physical.

Do That Relaxing Thing

Let your body relax until you can't feel it. Continue to repeat this notion in your head and stay focused. Don't allow yourself to give up. Say it out loud slowly if that helps.

"I will have an out of body experience. I will let myself go to sleep, but I will take this waking consciousness everywhere I go. I will leave my body with complete awareness."

Continue repeating this even after you become tired, and all you want to do is roll over.

If it helps you to stay comfortable then you can roll over, and continue to do it. If you begin to experience sensations or notice lights, ignore them and don't be worried. These will naturally happen. If you start to become too tired to remember what to say, shorten it to "mind awake, body asleep." Continue until you lose consciousness.

Whichever one of these techniques you pick, you will like not see any results the first time, or even the first couple of times. Take it slowly, and don't become frustrated when things don't happen. You will begin to see some results with time. You might have a physical or mental block that is preventing you from getting out of your body. You may have some past trauma, a bad diet, or an unhealthy pineal gland that you need to deal with. It could be a lot of different things.

Don't worry if you don't remember any details about your astral travels. You must write them down after you have finished your travel. When you are half asleep, everything seems obvious, and you think you will remember it forever. You might be so comfortable you want to fall asleep. Stand up and write down the details, you can

reconstruct the information later.

The important thing here is not what you do but why you do it. This applies to your thoughts. Just think about it. You need to be completely honest with yourself. Cleanse your mind from all garbage and never follow the flock.

How far can you go in this universe? There are no limits.

Chapter 10: Your Divine Self

The divine self is the inner life force. This is your true motivation for living. The divine self-powers you and cause you to wonder. It is the light at your core that chose to be incarnate a certain point in time.

The divine self is always aware. It has been thinking and aware since you were born in this lifetime and every other lifetime. The physical realm and body that we dwell in is just what holds your higher self.

You chose to be here, and that's why you are here. This energy force of awareness and life provides you with lessons that have to be learned, and exchanges need to be made that you are only about to do as a human.

It might seem like the rules of incarnation, birth, living in this busy world, would prevent us from knowing our diving self which lives within our core. This doesn't have to be true. You can choose it do be a different way.

We can acknowledge our divine core and start to draw our self even closer to our higher being.

The first thing you have to do is to embrace your divine self.

Let your mind shut off as you quiet and calm yourself.

Get rid of distractions. No music, clocks, telephones, children, lawnmowers, television, or radios.

Sit comfortably and chose a mirror or candle.

If you chose a candle, stare into the flame. If you want to use a mirror, start at it and look over your entire face. Make sure you don't look into your eyes, and don't allow the flame to cause your eyes to go out of focus

Stay aware of yourself. Remain in your body and keep yourself relaxed. Keep your eyes focused.

The candle flame represents the light that is all life force. Everything that is alive is powered by light. All things that are real is perceivable by the absorption and reflection of light. Light is all that is.

The mirror reflects an image of self that is both avoided and embraced.

We stay away from it because we tend to want to compare it to beauty or perfect that we expect to find within the natural world. We stay away from imperfections of the body because they make use think we are unlovable and unworthy.

People don't realize that life is about the imperfections. Conscious energy is perfect and wants to be incarnate, so it can experience the sorrow and joy that is a reality. It wants to experience sorrow and joy

that is imperfect and learn how to send our unconditional love in spite of these sorrows and imperfections.

This is the only time where you can learn true lessons and become closer to integrating with the All. The All is the Source or Creator. It isn't female or male but just is. All is presented the same way as everything else; it comes from its source. This means that everyone, awareness, and light is contantly present and everyone is siblings in this Light Family.

Something that we tend to miss is that the things and people that we assume are perfect have actually been changed to appear perfect and they're in no way natural. The thought of natural perfection is just a

lie

Another reason we embrace self is the ego; everybody understands that we have a body, and this body contains a shape, face, mouth, nose, and eyese. We believe this to be the truth because we are about to see and feel it.

When a person looks in a mirror, they will likely only see a physical thing, something that is made up of matter, like a candle or match. We may be matter, and we do decay and die, but there's more. We can feel anger, love, cry, make things with our hands, celebrate religions, reproduce, stay up late to think, and make choices.

Are we just matter? Are we not anything more like a personality incarnate or a spirit?

Thoughts and personality aren't just a physical function. They may be powered by a physical function, but this is only a bridge between you body and spirit. Gas powers a car through combustion which changes the gases state. The brain works to convert the spirit, but we need the spirit to fuel our life. When our engines becomes clogged, we only have to look for a neglected spirit to find the reason.

Being looking at your reflection in the mirror as not something that is just bone and flesh, but also as a spiritual being that moves within your body. Then you will develop the connection that you have to things that are beyond the physical realm.

Third Eye Awakening

Take a moment to look at your reflection. Notice your bodies light and the life glow that surrounds it.

While doing this either with the mirror or candle, embrace the energy of creation, the light of life, and your connection to it all. Say this affirmation, "I believe in myself. I know it because I feel it in me. I can see it in my life."

Repeat this and don't be mindless. Repeat as you feel this truth in your heart. Take note of the divine energy and the connection with the universe and the buzz of creation on your skin.

Continue to repeat this, or change it to suit you. Think about the divine self and then try to make contact with the manifesting self

Make sure you stay open to the divine self and keep the heart open to be able to communicate with the higher being and see how your life happens.

Do this with the cycle of the moon. This is best during a new moon. Continue doing this for as long as you feel you need to so that you can build up your relationship with your higher being, and to come closer to understanding.

At the mystical heart of all religions is the higher self. Understanding the higher self is the most important thing that anyone can have.

The higher self is seen as a relationship with the evolving self on the Chart of Your Divine Self. I show many cosmic truths that were discovered by great mystics of the West and East.

The Chart has three parts that can be called your identity's trinity.

There is an upper figure where a sphere of light resides. The Hindus call this Brahma. Buddhists call it Dharmakaya and Christians think of it as the Heavenly Father. It is God's spirit that has been individualized for everyone.

Your higher self is surrounded by seven spheres that make up your body. These spheres of energy contain all your good works. This is your cosmic bank account.

Your body has spheres of cosmic consciousness that include seven planes of heaven and seven spheres of awareness that correspond with the seven days of creation, the seven Archangels, the seven Elohim, and the seven colors that come from the white light that is the Father.

These seven ways lead to seven paths that go back to the Source. The lords of the seven rays are masters who teach on these paths.

Your higher self is a part of you right now. It will never be removed.

It is not separate from you in space or time. The only separation that you have from your higher self is your consciousness, your limitations, and the vibrations you have accumulated from this life and previous ones that are less than your highest qualities.

Between the light above and the soul below is the higher self. The higher self is a part of you that translates an imperfect soul into

perfection. It is a portion of you that is real and can stand within the presence of your God.

Some Christians refer to your higher self as the inner heart of the man.

It is your higher self that helps you come through your evolutions and all your experiences in space and time.

Depending on your religion, you can think of this higher self as a guardian angel, voice of conscience, your inner guru, and of course your closest friend.

What the Chart show is that all of us has a higher self and everyone is destined to be one with the higher self. It doesn't matter if we call it Atman, Tao, Buddha, or Christ.

Your soul evolves on a spiritual path in space and time. It is part of the mortal you, but it can become immortal.

The violet flame is a presence that surrounds you. This flame is an energy that has a high frequency and forgives. It is a spiritual alchemy.

There is a protective white light known as God around the violet flame. We apply the spoken word to call forth the light as protection. It will seal our chakras and aura from the weight of darkness.

The white light that descends from God to the higher self is a silver cord or the umbilical cord. It is the lifeline that connects you to the Spirit.

This silver cord nourishes a radiant flame of God that is closed inside

the secret chamber in the heart. This is a threefold flame that carries the attributes of love, wisdom, and power.

It is a very spiritual flame that is about 1/16th of an inch and focused in the body at heart. It is a sacred fire that God has moved from his heart to yours.

Your soul's evolution is ascended to the light, fulfill your mission, balance your karma, and grow in self-mastery.

The end of your incarnations is becoming the real self so you can return to the spiritual dimension that is your real home. By paying attention to your spiritual path, the figures on the chart that are separated due to a limited consciousness will eventually become one.

You can attain a union with God.

Chapter 11: Trust Your Intuition

A little voice in your head. A tingle. An urge. These are gut feelings talking to you. What are they saying and do you need to listen?

Many have experienced a sense of knowing something before we know them. You wait at a green light and miss getting hit by a car that ran a red light. You decide out of the blue to go on a blind date, and you find the love of your life.

If we could just tap into these insights, we would be better. Guess what? You can. If you can learn to identify what signals to listen to. It might be butterflies in your tummy, a certainty that something is about to happen, or sweaty palms.

Intuition is more material than it seems. The intuitive right brain is reading your surrounding while the left brain is engaged in something else. The body registers this information while the mind remains unaware of what is going on.

Theory suggests that you might feel an event approaching due to dopamine neurons. Dopamine keeps track of reality and alerts us to patterns that we can't consciously detect.

Just how do you choose what gut feeling to trust? That is a matter of combining the intuition and the mind and getting the right balance between rational thinking and gut instinct. When you notice an intuitive hit, you can engage your mind to weigh the choices and figure out how to act on them.

Here are some gut feelings that experts recommend you pay attention to:

Something Feels Wrong with Your Body

Listen to your body's signals is the crucial part of exercising your intuitive sense. Your body is a wonderful communicator. Intuition can allow you to get warning signs when something is off with your body so you can take care of it. If you have a feeling about your body like something is toxic or weak, listen to it. Get it looked at. Many people ignore this sense when something isn't right, and then they find out that something small has become large.

Physical symptoms have symbolic values. If you are near someone and your energy level goes down, don't ignore this intuition. Sleepiness can mean that you are near an energy draining circumstance or person. It might be your body's way of telling you that the conditions are draining your energy. If you stay in this situation that makes you feel depleted, it can lead to situations where you could become stuck, anxious, and depressed.

Pay attention to any physical sensation that happens suddenly during an interaction. You might get a burning sensation in your stomach before deciding not to get in a cab and moments later the driver gets arrested for theft. You can feel intuitions in most parts of your body. Most feel them in their stomach or chest. The stomach is more common since the intestine house the enteric nervous system referred to as the second brain.

You Feel Like You Are in Danger

The feelings you get from someone in the first ten seconds you meet them is an ancient biological wisdom. Early humans that could detect quickly if a stranger was a foe or friend and had a better survival rate. Their descendants could read emotional signals in other's faces instantly.

Since social conditioning can help create beliefs and these beliefs can produce impressions and decisions that are flawed. Check your gut feelings with your rational mind when you can. There are ways you can take care of what feels like warnings.

If you feel you can't trust someone, you need to pay attention to that feeling. If you are walking alone and you feel like you need to stay away from the person coming toward you, cross the street or change your path.

You Want to Help

Our gut instincts have been developed to help us avoid danger, but we have evolved so much that we have the capability to sense when a friend needs help. Sympathy is a basic instinct. This is why evolution gave attention to the parts of the brain that make us think about other people's feelings.

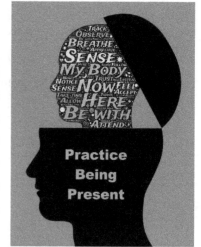

Third Eye Awakening

Evolution has enabled you to be able to read faces and signals, so you don't have to wait to be asked before you reach out to help. The smallest gesture can make a huge difference in someone's day. People are more compelled to give after they see pictures of people after a disaster rather than just reading about it.

The ability to read other's faces doesn't just help others. Generosity makes the brain's pleasure center light up as bright as the Las Vegas strip.

Individuals that help others experience improvements in overall well-being, immunity, and mood. Following your instincts for generosity and sympathy is a good investment for your happiness and health, too.

You Know What You Are Doing

There are things in your life that you have problems with. You have cooked a certain dish for what seems like forever but when you mother-in-law is coming to dinner, your brain shuts off, and you forget what to do. The can-do instinct that has been developed over the years gets drowned out by overthinking.

Beginning golfers do better when they think about their putts. Experienced golfers do worse when the start thinking about what they are doing. Rational thinking does serve beginners since they are still developing technique and muscle memory. For experienced players, their natural instinct took over, and they did a better job. Overriding their neural patterns and instincts for logical thought destroyed their performance.

When you get tempted to think too much about something that you know how to do, try some distraction. When your yoga instructor call out that dreaded pose that eludes you, say the alphabet backward or sing your favorite song to yourself. Engaging your mind with something else will leave your instincts free to do what they do.

This Feels Right

When your intuition says that you have found someone or something that is right for you, the choice will become very easy. It will feel good and won't feel like you are forcing anything.

When you need to make a large decision that will have lasting

repercussions, you need to let your gut decide. Using our gut instincts to make big decisions leads to choices that are more satisfying. These decisions will improve your quality of life.

Here are some ways to trust and uncover your intuition:

Release Your Core Beliefs

All of us carry core beliefs. These were formed from the time of birth and continue to change with interactions, environment, circumstances that we experienced growing up. These beliefs want to rule us. It seems like we are strapped beside our alter ego that is determined to take us down, all while we are begging it to stop.

Identify what you think about yourself, move and feel through all the negativity, the pain and accept all that happened along the way. This allows you to go forward and trust your intuition.

Turn Loose of Childhood Hurts

Like most people, childhoods are perfect. There are some good memories and bad ones, too. As you get older, you will look back and realize how hard it was for your parents to raise you.

You will learn to accept and love your parents for who they are and be grateful for everything they did for you. Stop blaming your parents for your adult choices. Do what it takes to let go of all the childhood hurts. If you can't or won't, it is only going to hold you back in everything you try to do. It will stop your ability to trust your intuition.

Listen to Your Gut

Intellectually all of us know that this means to follow that little voice in your heart or head. Listen to your gut because the answer will be within you.

This sounds simple, but for some, it will be developed with time. Allow yourself to move forward and change. Don't wallow in self-doubt. There are probably times you can remember where you didn't listen to your gut and you chose a different path.

Your choices probably didn't give you good results, and then you wasted time blaming yourself for making a stupid decision. Trust your gut. It will never lead you wrong.

Meditate in Strange Places

You could begin with walking meditation if you like being outdoors. You could sit quietly on a cushion and enjoy the start of your day. You can sneak in a quick meditation on the subway or sit in a doctor's office. Take time to meditate while your dog is enjoying

friends at a dog park.

The wonderful thing about meditating is the space that you can find in between. That space where one thought ends and the next hasn't quite begun. You can rejuvenate, reflect, and rest in this quiet, natural space. This space is where compassion, clarity, and understanding is nurtured and born. This is a safe place where you can get to know yourself. You can sit still and listen to what is inside. Regular meditation will keep your intuition present and fresh.

Forgive Self-harm

Everyone has a form of self-harm like boozing, isolating, or over-indulging. The biggest harm we cause ourselves if stay stuck in our beliefs that we aren't worthy. If you can walk away from self-harm, you can begin to let down your guard that wants to punish you. When you start to look at yourself with forgiveness and compassion, you will fill that space with mindfulness and love.

You can start to tap into your gut at a deeper level.

Break All Bonds of Resentments and Attachments

If you find it hard to get rid of anything, you are hanging on the feelings that are attached to bad feelings like resentment and anger. This will only allow those feelings to grow and fester.

When you release your grip on attachments and resentments, you are giving yourself permission to let go completely. You will start to make a space where you can relax and learn to trust yourself. You will start to rely on and listen to your intuition.

Come Home to Yourself

It is way too easy to get into a bad habit of compulsively rushing, seeking, and searching for something just to keep yourself distracted from feeling uncomfortable. Stop running away and begin to run to yourself. Trust yourself to hold the answers. Once you can feel at home with yourself, you will start to feel safe in the world. You will begin to pay attention and listen to your intuition.

Wherever you are at is perfect.

Every one of us is a work in progress. It will take practice, patience, and willing to find self-discovery. When you awaken and connect to your intuition, anything will be possible.

Chapter 12: Personal Meditation

The meditations in this chapter will help you connect with yourself better, and will help you to become more in tune with yourself. This will aid in your ability to connect with your divine and higher self. When you are more connected with yourself, the easier it will be for you to trust your intuition. You're not going to doubt someone that you are close with; the same goes for yourself. Let's begin.

Sleep Meditation

The length of this meditation depends on how many times you have to do it before you begin to fall asleep. Some may be able to do it only once; others may have to go through it a couple of times.

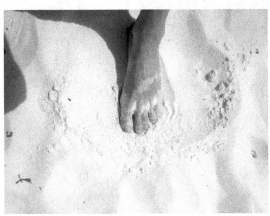

Take notice of how your body feels lying down, and take note of sensations throughout; lightness, heaviness, itchiness, tension, movement, heat, coolness, pressure, temperature, or tingling.

Notice these sensations without judging any of them, or without fighting them. Relax and continue to breathe deeply in through your nose and out through your mouth.

Now change your awareness to different areas of your body beginning with your right thumb. Notice any sensation in this area. If there isn't any sensation, notice the lack of a sensation and then move to the index finger. Repeat this process for every finger on your right hand, and then the complete right hand.

Now take your attention to your wrist, then up to the forearm, the elbow, the upper arm, the shoulder, the armpit, and the right side of your body. In all of these areas notice the sensations or lack thereof.

If any thoughts come up, acknowledge them and then allow them to be release, like a cloud floating across the sky.

Now take your thoughts to your left hand, up your arm, your shoulder, and the left side of your body. Observe everything you feel in each area as you did on the right side. Acknowledge and pay attention to these sensations. Don't try to figure out why they are there or understand them, just notice them.

Keep your breath a normal rate.

Now focus your attention on your right buttock and notice it's sensations. Move down your right leg to your thigh, then onto your knee, then the calf, the shin, the ankle, foot, and then the toes.

As you did on the right, trace down your left leg for sensations starting with your left buttock.

Third Eye Awakening

Make sure you are staying completely relaxed. If you notice any area of your body is tensed, breathe into it and allow the tension to dissolve away. Take your focus to your back; tingling, heat, coolness, pressure, or any other kind of movement.

Move your attention to the front of the body and focus on your stomach, up your chest, and then around your neck.

Lastly, focus on your chin, up to your cheeks, your nose, both eyes, eyelids, right eyebrow, left eyebrow, both temples, your forehead, back of the head, sides of your head, and your crown.

Relax for a moment. Rest in the new awareness you have created. Continue your breath as normal. Scan through your body again, but in bigger clusters, right then left arm, then both arms together, right then left leg, then both legs together, stomach, chest, neck, and your head.

Then scan your body as a whole. Continue this same process, starting from the beginning with just your right thumb, until you feel yourself starting to relax into sleep.

Repeat this as many times as you need to.

Laughter Meditation

This meditation is a more advanced meditation. This typically takes about 12 minutes and is made up of three separate parts; stretching, laughter, and stillness. This meditation should be done first thing in the morning on an empty stomach. If that doesn't work for you, make sure you do this right before lunch or dinner.

Begin by stretching out your body. Stand on your toes and interlace your fingers. Your arms above your with your palms facing up, keeping the fingers intertwined. Slowly release.

Stretch and loosen your face and jaw muscles. Yawning is a perfect way to do so.

Begin you laughter by turn the corners of your mouth up into a soft smile. Let your smile grow and then begin laughing without using any force.

Start to deepen you laughter so that you can feel it coming up from your belly. Try to laugh with yourself, or a partner if you are doing this with a friend. Do not laugh about or at something or someone.

Be mindful while you are laughing. Notice everything your experience at this moment. Continue your laughter for five minutes.

Once your five minutes are up, stop laughing and gently close your eyes. Allow your body to become still and find a comfortable spot to sit if chose to stand while you were laughing.

Notice the silence around. Ignore the thoughts that may come and shift your attention to your sensations and feelings in the body.

Higher-Self Meditation

This meditation will help you to connect with your higher self. This meditation can take up to 30 minutes to complete, so make sure you have plenty of time set aside.

Start by focusing your attention on your breath. Take a deep, slow breath in and allow your stomach to expand out. Slowly exhale and allow your body to relax with your exhale completely.

Allow the mind to become still and relaxed. If any thoughts come up while in this meditation, in your mind, simply say "silence now."

Allow your eyes to close and imagine yourself relaxing under a large tree. The branches of the trees extend out high above you, reaching towards the light in the sky. This is just like the network of branches that connects you to your higher self's light.

Picture a gorgeous golden angel standing before you; this is your high self, and who you are. As you take in this angel, it glows with light and smiles at you. Ask your angel, your higher self, to combine with you.

Picture a part of your higher self as a golden ball falling and sinking into your body as you are sitting under the large tree. Feel this ball entering into your crown chakra.

A part of your higher self-has now become one with your consciousness. You now also have a permanent golden light that connects you to your higher self. Now check in with your higher self, and see what it wants to tell you. Ask your higher self any questions if you have something that you need an answer to.

Let your mind sit still and wait for words, images, or impressions to enter your mind. Your higher self can communicate with your through instant knowing, pictures, or words. This will change and evolve the more of connection you have with your higher self.

You have now completed your first step in connecting with your higher self. The more you practice, the easier this will become, and your connection will become stronger. Every day, clear your mind and connect with your higher self when you need guidance.

Now is the time to leave your meditation. Gently bring your mind back to the body. Wiggle your toes and fingers and once your mind and body feel ready, slowly open your eyes and come back to consciousness.

Chapter 13: Clearing Out Negative Energy

We live in a world of twos just like it was intended. There is good and bad and right and wrong. The yin and yang theory exists inside  and out. This is the reason why the earth's plane is a great school for the soul's expansion. It there wasn't duality, we wouldn't have growth, variety, joy, or pain.

This means that the energies and people we come in contact with offer us lessons that we need while on our path here. This might just point to learning how to clear, protect, and work with negative energy. It could easily be compared to a video game.

Anyone can feel the effects of lower energies during times of transition and high stress. We sometimes absorb, receive, or attract lower energies from the people in our environment. This is all part of the game, and these experiences will help us expand as souls and individuals.

Here are some signs to know that negative energy has latched onto you:

- You might get calls dropped or static on your phone when speaking to someone where you normally get a good connection.

- You might begin feeling depressed, and you have never been diagnosed with depression.
- You can't log into your bank or other online accounts, and you just get an error message, and you know your internet is strong.
- You get tired quickly and feel like you need a nap even though you  slept fine the night before.
- You restrain from helping yourself like eating even though you are hungry.
- You have a sore throat and feel like you have the flu.
- You lose your wallet or keys, have something stolen, lock your keys in the car.
- Your email didn't get to who it was intended for, and then you get fussed at for not emailing them.
- Your mind begins to spin on negative thoughts about something or someone from your past. You try hard to shake them off, and they just stick to you like glue.
- Your behavior begins to be against self-love like spending too much money on unnecessary things especially if you don't have the money for it. This is important if this isn't your normal character.

There are endless possibilities, so it is up to all of us to recognize and notice these patterns since they are personal. It might take you years to see what is happening when you get affected by negative energy. If you experience a combination of these all in one day, or in a short time span, this can help you realize what is happening. It will become clearer as you begin to tune into your awareness.

Third Eye Awakening

When you realize you that you have picked up negative energies, there are several methods you can use either alone or together to help clear your energy field, body, and mind of this negativity. The reverse is true even if it was unintentional.

The world houses many people. Every person has their desires and intentions. Some are positive while others are negative. While others tend to embrace negativity completely.

It isn't possible to remove every negative person from your life. They might be coworkers or possibly family.

It isn't possible to change these people either. This leaves you in a

predicament, especially if you are a sensitive empath. There is hope; you can get out of that predicament without having to change others but changing what is inside you.

Here are some ways that you can clear this negativity:

Declare you are getting rid of this energy: By stating your intentions out loud has incredible power.

This simple act makes them real. Making them exist instead of just being an idea. When you have decided that all the negative energy around you is enough and you want to reduce it, start by saying it aloud. You don't have to tell anyone. Just get it out there and let your voice come back to your ears. Take the intention and go forward to make it happen.

Yawn: Yes, do it. Many think that yawning is a sign of discontentment or boredom, it clears the body of unwanted energy. This should not be a surprise since breathing can reduce anxiety. Yawning is just a strong purpose filled breath.

Smudge: An unpleasant person spent the weekend with you, and now your place feels heavy with negative energy. You may feel as though you have brought too much stress home from work. In either scenario, a smudging might be what you need. In smudging ceremonies, white sage has been used for hundreds of years to get rid of unwanted spirits and energies.

Say a Mantra: This takes the declaring your intention one step more and lets you order the negative energy out.

Repeat this: I, (state your name), do not give permission for any non-physical or living being to come into my body, energy field, spirit, soul, and mind for anything other than love.

Third Eye Awakening

I break all agreements, vows, and contracts that I may have made unknowingly in any dimension, space, and time that will diminish the expression of my joyful soul.

I break all agreements from this point in time and backward through all experiences in my past, and forward till the end of time.

I order these people and energies to leave this space NOW! You no longer have power over me. I ask for protection from these energies so that they won't return to my energy field. I build a shield of light around me with this intention and my free will. I thank you that it's done. (end)

Say this mantra as many times as you need to.

Laugh: There is a reason that laughter is called the best medicine. It triggers a change in your body that boosts positive energy and reduces stress and pain. You might feel weird to laugh at nothing. Just do it. Within moments, your laugh will be genuine.

Get a Himalayan salt lamp: Himalayan salt lamp cleanses the air around it and will increase positive energy. It produces negative ions that grab positive ones the exude negativity. It sounds counter-intuitive, but the results are great. There are many different salt lamps.

Dance: Your brain releases endorphins every time you dance. This creates a positive field around you. It also talks about the universe. Joy is a high form of vibration. This places you on a plane that negativity can't reach.

Change your karma: When you are faced with negative energy, you might be tempted to dish it right back at them. This accomplishes nothing. It will set you back and causes more energy to build up. Engage in acts of kindness. Help someone less fortunate. Donate to your favorite charity. Volunteer your time at a food pantry. These acts will reduce the negative energy and boost your karma.

Spend time with someone special: If you are in a relationship, having sex can help get rid of negative energy and replace it with positive. Other things will happen when two people have sex like lowering blood pressure, boosting your immune system, and stress relief.

Create a negative collector: Set a glass on water on a table or light a candle. While looking at it declare your intent to get all the negative energy into the water or flame. This will also get rid of pain and emotional problems.

Go Green: Plants are a great filter for negative energy. Place on in every room that you spend time in. Open windows and let the sunlight in is another good cleaner.

Claim the space: If you place feels like it is full of other people's stuff, walk around and claim it. Once you have installed positive energy, the negative energy that hangs around won't be able to stay.

Salt: Sprinkle salt on your carpets. Let it sit for about an hour and then vacuum. Salt has a natural ability to absorb negative energy.

You can also put out bowls of salt in the corners of each room. Let it sit for a few hours and then remove it.

Room Spray: Make a room spray with essential oils that will clear out negative energy. The best ones to use are patchouli, frankincense, lavender, and rose. This will work on people, too. Just mist yourself gently.

High-frequency music: Playing music with high vibrations will make a big difference. We know that music makes a difference in our energy. It does the same thing for spaces.

Black Tourmaline: This crystal can clear negative energy. This crystal doesn't need to be cleared as others crystals do. This can work for people, as well. Just put on in your purse or pocket when traveling. It is good for sensitive people who pick up on energy and need protection.

Clean your office or home: You need to unclutter. Old things trap negative energy. You need to get rid of documents, magazines, newspapers, and old clothes. Clean your house. Don't just vacuum and do the dishes. Clean the laundry, windows, walls, curtains, and rugs. Open the windows and let the fresh air in. Make your office or home a positive space, and you will notice all the negative energy leave.

Change the way you think: Clean your negative thoughts. Don't allow small problems to bother you. Don't criticize or judge others and try not to complain. Love yourself more. Forgive yourself. No one is perfect. Don't dwell on imperfections or mistakes. Say positive affirmations daily to help you make your thoughts positive. Motivating and inspiring quotes do the same thing. Keep a gratitude journal. Take a few minutes each day to write what you are thankful for. Don't pretend to be a victim. You have created your life so take the responsibility. Stop putting the blame on others and take steps to make your life better.

Take a bath: Take a hot shower or bath can help elevate your energy. This is very easy. Just soak about 20 to 30 minutes to unwind and relax. You can also add some sea salt or essential oils to your bath. Salt baths are a great way to cleanse your aura and increase your vitality and health.

Put your worries on paper: Write down everything that worries you. It might seem like it's huge, but when you see it on paper, you will understand that it isn't much at all and you can handle it. The reason behind this is to take the negative energy from inside you and put it on paper. Don't make this list short. Try to write down all of your negative thoughts. Every worried thought that you are having. Then get rid of the paper. Throw it away or burn it.

Meditate: Mediation increases your serotonin and improves your behavior and mood. It will decrease anxiety, helps gain peace of mind and clarity. It will help heal your energy system and keep a vibrant energy field. Choose a peaceful environment. Lie or sit down comfortable and clear your mind. Meditation isn't complicated.

Visualize: If you are worried about something, visualize the outcome as positive. Envision the result in your mind, so you won't have to worry about it anymore. Imagine how it will make you feel and keep that feeling for as long as you can. If nothing is worrying you, but  you still feel negative, visualize a dream that makes you happy.

Work it out: When nothing else is working, and you still feel sad or angry, the best thing you could do is sweat it out. Exercise is a great way to battle anxiety, depression, and stress. Whatever you choose to do, tennis, walking, swimming, lifting weights, yoga, running, a great workout can clean your mind of negative thoughts.

Chapter 14: Use Your Mind to Heal

Over the last few decades, a revolution has happened with how we see the body. What looks just like an object, an anatomical structure, is a process, which is a constant flow of information and energy. Think about this; at this moment, your body is switching things around, shuffling and exchanging its molecules and atoms with everything in the universe. This is being done at a speed faster than you can change your clothes. Actually, the body your have right now, at this very second, is different than the body you had when you work, or even from a few minutes ago.

All of the cells in your body are in constant communication with each other so that they can fight off diseases and infections, eliminate toxins, digest food, keep your heart beating, and several other functions that help to keep you alive. These processes probably seem like that are out of conscious control, a lot of research has found that there is nothing that holds more power over your body than your mind.

When you think, you are using brain chemistry. When you

experience an emotion, thought, or feeling, you are creating a neuropeptide. These molecules travel through the body and connect with receptor neurons and cells. The brain uses information, turns it into chemicals, and then tells the entire body that there is either cause for celebration or trouble. The body is directly affected as the neuropeptides flow through the bloodstream, sharing the energetic effect of what the brain is currently feeling and thinking.

When a person says their heart is happy, then they have have a happy heart. If a person were to look inside that heart, they would find being affected by the molecules that cause happiness and joy, like large amounts of serotonin and dopamine. If a person was excessively sad, their skin could be examined and they would find large amounts cortisol.

To be able to harness the unlimited power of your mind you have to expand your self-awareness. When self-awareness is closed, then the flow of information and energy through the body-mind is hindered. This causes people to stay in toxic emotions like self-pity, regret, and resentment. Bad habits like not exercising or overeating tend to take hold. The loop of feedback between your body and mind will turn negative, and stress will either grind away at your daily life or your feel it hit instantaneously.

At the other end of things, when self-awareness is open, energy can flow freely. You are more creative, flexible, and balanced. You see the world and yourself with understanding and compassion. You become open to new things, and you have more energy. With this level of awareness, you have the power to create yourself a new reality, a reality that is full of vibrant well-being and health.

There are lots of different ways you can expand your awareness, which includes mindfulness and meditation. A self-aware approach to your life would include:

- Don't fear the future or regret the past. These will only bring out misery with self-doubt

- Redefine yourself each and every day

- Don't keep any secrets; they cause shadows in the psyche

- Become emotionally free, being resilient, emotionally, is a better defense than being rigid

- Work through blocks such as guilt and shame; they will falsely color reality

- Be responsible for all your conscious choices

- Examine all points of view as if they were your own

- Don't let denial censor incoming data

- Don't allow the feedback loop to be shut down by prejudices, judgment, or rigid beliefs

- Remain as open to input as you can be

- Be passionate about your experiences and your life

With that in mind, let's look at how housing that power can help you to heal yourself. A 37-year woman from Hungary was diagnosed with breast cancer, but she didn't want to use conventional treatment. The doctors suggested removing her breasts, but she didn't want to have to go through that. She felt that the answer was inside of her. She turned to things like reflexology and reiki before learning about German new medicine. German new medicine taught her that cancer was caused by the emotional conflict. Unfortunately, these things didn't work for her, and cancer started to spread. She then made her way to Lourdes looking for a cure.

Let's stop for a second. The knowledge of the mind being able to heal you isn't harmless. When these claims are made without any evidence, it can cause false hope, and if a person chooses to completely reject conventional treatment, they could die.

This makes it not so surprising that skeptics write off healing thoughts as evil and a threat to humanity that needs to be gotten rid of. They like to brand it as a placebo effect or quackery. But the thing is, these claims have no scientific proof either. While the mind may not be able to heal you completely, use of conventional medicine will likely be needed; there is growing evidence that the mind does influence your physical health.

You state of mind plays a big part in the effects of things like depression, fatigue, nausea, and pain. Burn patients find a 50% better reduction in pain by using virtual reality games instead of painkillers. Placebo medications work through the mind. The mind expects the medication to do something, which causes the release of dopamine and other healing chemicals.

If you are having trouble believing that your body has this kind of power, consider these examples from medical literature:

- A group veterans that were plagued by severe osteoarthritis were able to regain pain-free mobility after they had shame surgery. The surgeon made a small incision on their knees and sewed the incisions back up, but did nothing to their knees.

- A woman that had suffered from depression was so impressed at how well her depression had lifted that she thought she was in the active drug group. She later found out that she was in the placebo group.

- A man had been diagnosed with incurable cancer and died not long after, but his autopsy showed that he had been misdiagnosed.

The key to being able to tap into this power is through mental rehearsal. This is where you picture the desired outcome in a way that causes your inner thoughts to be more real than what is around you. If you can combine a clear intention of what it is you want along with a positive emotion, gratitude, and joy, you can give your body a taste what could possible happen, but in the present moment.

If you can make this visualization feel real enough, the brain won't be able to distinguish the difference and will fire up some new neurons and create connections until things begin to appear as if this event has taken place. In a quantum physics standpoint, all of your possibilities exist in the current moment, so you pick a new future from these infinite possibilities, and you are successful in your use of mental rehearsal to make it feel real enough times, it is possible to observe your new future into reality by changing your DNA.

This means you become somebody new because the body and the brain won't identify with who you used to be. In this way, you have

become your placebo. This can work for anybody. There is no need to be a spiritual master or a neuroscientist for this to work.

To help get you on the right track, here are seven ways to get your mind working for your body:

1. Help your treatments work by expecting them to work

This goes back to how effective the placebo effect can be. If you are told that a pill can cure your headache, the treatment is more likely to be helpful, even if the pill doesn't have any medicinal qualities. If you go to a chiropractor for back pain or a physical therapist for a bad knee, you have to believe that these treatments are going to help for them to be effective.

2. Keep a gratitude journal for better sleep

If you have a problem with insomnia, using a gratitude journal may be able to help. Studies have found that gratitude is linked to better quality and longer sleep. Right before bed, write down three things that you are grateful for. Coming up with these feelings of thankfulness before you go to sleep will increase your odds of a better night's sleep.

3. Focus on your life's purpose and live longer

If you feel that you have a purpose in life, then you have a greater chance of living longer. Research has found that people that believe that their lives are purposeful live a longer and healthier life. This

could mean that you find purpose in your life, or you find meaning in volunteering for your community, make sure that you do something that matters to you. Give yourself a reason to want to hop out of bed every day.

4. Keep optimistic, and your immunity will receive a boost

Lots of research has found that people who are optimistic are a lot less likely to become sick. For a long time they believed optimistic people just took better care of themselves, but recently they have found that the hopeful outlook is what boosts their immunity. When you look on the bright side of things, you are less likely to have a cold or an infection because your immune system can perform at its peak efficiency.

5.   Meditation slows aging

Meditation can provide you with a buffer from the effects that stress has on your body. Meditation is also able to slow your rate of cellular aging. This means you can stay looking more youthful, and avoid age-related diseases through meditation. Research has found that if you teach children to meditation, it will provide them with lifelong benefits. It doesn't matter what age you are thought. It's never too late to receive health benefits with meditation.

6.   Imagine yourself working out, and you can build muscles

Wouldn't it be great if you could become buff by just imagining yourself lifting weights? This may be possible because research has

found that using mental imagery can help you to gain muscle growth without ever lifting a finger. One particular study has found that people who pictured themselves lifting weights had a 24% increase in muscle strength. The people that lifted weights had better results, but the research still shows that mental training works and results in changes.

7.   Laughing will reduce heart disease

If you want to have a healthier heart, then start thinking about something that will make you laugh. Laughter can decrease stress hormones and increase your good cholesterol, as well as reducing artery inflammation. The effects of laughter will last 24 hours after you laugh.

Your mind can be your worst enemy or your best asset. Start training your brain so that it can help your body to perform at its best. Everybody can build their mental strength. With a little bit of practice, mental exercises may just be the key to living a happier and longer life.

Chapter 15: Psychic Awareness

Psychic awareness is completely real if you haven't figured that out so far. Celebrities like Kelsey Grammer, Jennifer Aniston, and Demi Moore have all said publicly that psychic awareness is an important part of their everyday life. Business icons like Bill Gates and Henry Ford have said that it was the helping hand to their biggest achievements.

Recently psychic awareness has become more mainstream. This isn't something that is only found in new age shops or on psychic hotlines on late night TV. Even scientists have started talking about psychic awareness, and the CIT has admitted that they have been exploring this.

Individually, psychic ability is there to help you to avoid suffering, to help you make the best decision, and help you to see the path your need to take to achieve everything you want in life. It's present to help make your life more peaceful, more exciting, and more joyful.

Everybody has the ability to develop psychic abilities. It's an innate and natural ability that only needs to be developed with some training and experience. Now, ask yourself, are you using and developing your psychic abilities? If you're not, then why? You could be missing out and denying yourself some of the best gifts available.

There are several excuses out there as to why people have chosen not to develop their psychic abilities. Some of the most common are:

- **Psychic abilities are evil**

This is commonly preached in religious viewpoints. But let me point in worries you may have at ease. Psychic abilities have nothing to do with evil things. This is a natural human ability that you have to tap into. There are no dark forces at play.

- **Only certain people have this ability**

This isn't true at all. Like I've said before, this is something that everybody can tap into. Psychic ability doesn't require any sort of special abilities.

- It takes years to develop fully

While it may try that you won't ever stop learning and working with your ability, it does not take intense training or years to develop. There are several different ways to develop your abilities. Some of these can take a few weeks, while others are slower and not as direct.

- Becoming psychic will turn me into a freak

 This maybe what TV shows and movies want you to think, but this isn't the case in real life. You won't act crazy, you won't see dead people, and you will be able to live a perfectly normal life. Yes, you can use this ability to tune into things that other people can't, but if you are trained properly, you will be able to keep this under control.

Now that we've covered some common reason of avoiding the development of psychic abilities let's move onto why should develop them.

First, you need to understand your channels of communication. Many often assume that psychic skills mean that you can see mental pictures, or you're clairvoyant. However, being able to see things is only one way of receiving information. Some people abilities come through as clairsentient, which means that they receive their guidance with feelings. You can also receive information through clairaudience, which is hearing a something either inside or outside of your mind. There's also claircognizance, which means you know chunks of information about something without having a reason to know. Everybody has a natural channel to receive their psychic guidance, along with a secondary channel. The important thing is to be open to all of these different channels.

Daily meditation is another important part of developing your psychic abilities. Research has found a strong connection with psychic abilities and meditation. Meditation has the ability to synchronize the wave patterns of both brain hemispheres. This allows for the flow of information from the right side of the brain into the left side of the brain.

Cleansing and balancing your chakras is also important. After you have become used to daily meditation, the next thing is to start opening your chakras, which act as psychic channels. This is done by performing a meditation that is specifically designed to balance your chakras.

Next, you need to be mentally attuned. This means that you have centered your awareness onto your higher self's connection with the source of love and knowledge. If your mind slips into the ego, then your readings will start to become unreliable and inconsistent. What's worse, you may become afraid and unhappy.

Create an atmosphere to live in that expands your abilities. The environment of your room can detract or contribute from your abilities. Research has found that people that were in distraction-free rooms were able to give better readings. These rooms also had soft background music, and they were dimly lit. It also helps if you are well rested and comfortable.

It also helps to pray. This doesn't mean you have to be a religious person and pray to a God, but prayer in general helps. Studies have found a correlation between prayer and telepathy. Prayer helps to work your psychic mind, so figure out a higher being to pray to and watch how your abilities will change.

Start using some of these methods to help you further develop your psychic abilities. Make sure that you are open to everything, and be prepared for amazing things to happen when you are.

Chapter 16: Healing Meditation

The meditations you will find in this chapter will help you to heal different aspects of your life. Since these meditations will be helping you to work through things, they can get tough. If at any point during either of the meditations you start to feel overwhelmed, take a moment and pause, take a few deep breaths, and come back to it once you are calm.

Anger Releasing Meditation

This meditation should take around 20 minutes, and is made to help you work through past events that may be causing your anger in the present.

Start by taking a few deep breaths. Be aware of your breaths as you inhale and exhale. Do a few breaths until you start to feel relaxed and centered.

While you are breathing in, the picture that you are breathing in white light, and when you breathe out, you're releasing all the anger and tension in your body. Now you find yourself in a movie theater. As the lights dim and the screen lights come on, you see a memory from your past begin to play on the screen.

This memory is one of when you felt anger or pain from somebody or something from your childhood. Let this movie continue to play from the movie projector. Let yourself watch this memory as it continues to play, but make sure you stay detached from the emotions as much as you can.

You take a glance around the theater, and you notice that there is somebody else in the room with yours. This is the same person that caused you pain in the past. They are also sitting and watching this memory play out. This person is getting to experience the pain that you suffered while the memory plays.

You notice that the person starts to cry and then asks you for your forgiveness. You start to feel emotional as you process through the trauma and hurt that this memory has brought up.

In this space, you feel space completely and you decide to walk over to this person that has hurt you. You let them know that all of this is in the past and that you will forgive them for all the pain that they have caused you.

The room starts to fill up with a violet light and covers you and the person, and completely takes away the pain and hurt that you are feeling. You are crying, and you're being healed at a very deep level. You embrace this person in a hug, which allows your heart to open even more.

You notice all of your layers of anger and pain come to the surface a release away from a very deep level. As the feelings come up, stay with them for as long as you need to, until they have been released.

The violet light changes into a healing green light. Picture this healing green light all around you and healing every layer of you. The green light slowly dims back to the dark room, and the screen turns to white. The lights *come back on.*

Once you feel ready, slowly and gently bring your thoughts back to your body. Wiggle your fingers and toes, and, once you're ready, slowly open your eyes and come back to consciousness.

Releasing Fears

This meditation will provide you with psychic protection and help you to break through anxious and fearful feelings. This meditation can take around 15 minutes.

Start by calling upon the light, God, the Archangel Michael, or whatever you view this to be. Take in a deep, cleansing breath, and exhale slowly and gently. Start to become aware of your breaths speed. When you breathe slowly and deeply, your mind and body will start to relax.

Take in another deep breath and release it slowly. Picture a violet light coming from the sky and entering into the crown of your head. Picture this light removing any negativity, or fear based energies. This violet light is calming all of the fear-based energy that could be affecting you at this moment.

Keep asking this light to calm your fears, whatever these fears may be. Your fear could manifest several ways; repetitive habits, phobias, or fears. Watch as this light change these fears into neutral energy.

After a few minutes, all your anxiety and fear will become more manageable. Ask this light to seal up your aura and picture the aura becoming strong and clear.

If, at this point, you are feeling fear, picture these fear-based energies bouncing off of your aura. These negative energies are not longer able to penetrate your body and aura.

Request that this light takes away all of the entities or energies that are not good for you. Ask that the energies are removed on a permanent basis. Lastly, picture this violet light sealing up your aura with protection and light so that the only energies that can enter your field are love-based.

Try to hold a joy or happy feeling in your heart. Let this feeling to grow out of your heart and travel through your aura and body. Thank this violet light for helping you when you needed it.

Remember that you have the power of free will. Spirits will respect this free will, and so you have to ask for their assistance when you need them. Once you are ready, slowly bring your mind back to the present by wiggling your fingers and toes. Slowly open your eyes when you are ready.

30 Minute Relaxation

Start by finding a relaxing and comfortable seated position. Let body completely relax. Take a deep breath in, and a slow breath out. Take another deep cleansing breath in, and as you release your breath, allow all of the tension to leave your body.

Notice how the relaxation is starting at the bottom of your feet. It could feel as if you are stepping into a bathtub full of warm water, or your feet could feel tingly, or they could just feel loose and calm. Let this sensation spread over both feet, and spread up to the ankles

Notice how this sensation is rising up over your ankles, and moving through your lower legs, up to the knees and then passing onto your upper legs. Let the relaxation continue to rise up through the body, moving up to the hips and pelvic girdle, up to your lower back and stomach, up to the upper back and chest.

Allow the upper arms to relax, and down through the elbows, the lower arms, and the wrist. Notice the sensation spreading through to your hands, palms, back of the hands, and each and every finger. The hands now feel relaxed, warm, and heavy.

Notice how your body continues to relax more as your collar bone area begins to widen and relax. Let the shoulders relax back slightly. Let the upper back relax, even more, the shoulders, and then the neck.

Allow the relaxation to move up to the chin, back of the head, mouth, cheeks, nose, and eyes. Notice how your eyelids are becoming relaxed and heavy. Feel how the eyebrows relaxing down, ears, and forehead. Notice how your forehead feels relaxed and cool.

Third Eye Awakening

Allow the relaxation to move up to the crown of your head. Now your whole body is feeling calm and relaxed. Take note of how the relaxation is now flowing through your whole body, all the way from your feet to your head.

Allow yourself to relax more as your spine completely relaxes. Beginning where your spine meets up with the base of your head, notice the relaxation, notice how the muscles give up their tension and completely relax.

Allow this relaxation to move down the spine, upper back, middle back, and lower back, to the base of the spine at the tailbone. Feel how all of the muscles within the back are completely relaxed. Notice how this relaxation feels as it pulses through your body.

Take a deep cleansing breath in and hold. Completely relax your muscles allow that held breath to flow slowly and gently out of your mouth or nose. Take another deep breath in, breathing in nice cleansing relaxation. Slowly release the breath, allow any tension that remains to be released.

Continue to slowly and smoothly breathe as you check your body for any tension that may remain. If you happen to notice some tension, turn your focus there. Direct your relaxing breath to flow to that area of your body, and allow it to carry away the tension.

Picture the air that you are breathing in can cleanse the body and take away any tension. Picture relaxation coming with every inhale, and as you exhale, picture the tension leaving your body. Now just sit, completely relaxed, and enjoy this sensation for a few minutes.

Now turn your attention back to your body, and think about the areas that need to be healed. Make a picture in your mind that represents your current state of being. Imagine any physical ailment that has been troubling yours. This could be an injury, pain, or illness. It could be something you have been diagnosed with or a problem that doesn't have an identity. Whatever you want to heal, picture this issue within in your mind.

Focus on the area in which this problem is currently present. It might be best if you think of this issue as a dark area in your body, and imagine a relaxed healing light. Watch as this light of relaxation flows all through your body, and direct this light to the dark area that you want to heal.

Picture the healing relaxation light touching, swirling, flowing into the edge of the dark areas that are present in the body. You may even see small parts of the dark area being taken away by this relaxation. Let these pieces be carried away as you take your next exhale.

Breathe in calm, health, and healing, and breathe out problems in the body, tension, and illness. Let this healing light of relaxation to swirl through all of your dark problem areas. Watch as these dark spots continue to grow smaller.

Watch these dark areas as they are completely overtaken by relaxation. Watch as the relaxation light makes these dark spots lighter and lighter, taking away all the things that are bad for your body.

Picture your immune system working hard to heal your body. Watch as cells travel to the areas of the body that needs them, working where they need to. Feel this energy moving through the body. Picture the body filled up

with this sense of relaxation

Watch as these problem areas are healed in your body. Watch as they became lighter and filled with healing relaxation. Feel as they take away the discomfort you have been feeling, healing your body.

Let your body be healed by itself. Take a deep cleansing breath in and exhale all the things that you do not need. Take in more relaxation and exhale the tension. Take a few minutes to relax and picture this healing process

working throughout your body. Feel confident in the fact that your body can heal itself, and feel at peace and calm.

At this moment you can choose to return to your regular state of consciousness and become alert, or can drift off to sleep. If you want to awaken, notice how your mind and body are beginning to notice your surroundings even more.

If you would like to go to sleep, feel the relaxation begin to deepen more. On the count of three, you will reach whichever desired a state of alertness or relaxation that you so desire. One, two, three.

Chapter 17: Clearing Out Your Energy Fields

Have you ever experienced a sudden onset of tiredness or heaviness for no real reason? You could have just caught onto somebody else's energetic field. This is caused by the principle of resonance. The trauma of your ancestors, other's emotions, or negative feng shui of rooms can mess up your energy field. This can create problems for you that include chronic illnesses, fatigue, and mild depression.

Everything in the world has a field of energy, and the energy needs to be maintained properly. Just like our bodies have to eliminate waste, the energy field of all things living needs to eliminate some energetic toxins. These types of energetic toxins aren't visible, and they can't be measured, but they still have the ability to affect us.

The hygiene of our energy fields is typically overlooked, even in holistic and alternative practices. The thing is though; it's extremely easy to do. There is not strength involved, and you don't have to gather or send energy. You don't have to manipulate energy; you're just working with information, much like working a computer program.

Let's look at some ways that you can clear out your energy fields so that you no longer have to suffer from the ill effects of a clogged energy field. These are especially helpful to empaths.

- Cut ties

While this one doesn't clear out your energy field necessarily, it will help to keep them from getting clogged. If you're an empath, you are probably really good at creating relationships, and people are naturally drawn to you. They take your energy, and they don't give anything back.

Present and past connections with people; lovers, friends, or family members will stay with you long after your relationship is over with them. Now is the time to cut those ties. You have to make a choice to do this; nobody else can do this for you.

To cut the ties, all you have to do is picture this person that you had a relationship with and picture the cords being cut. Bless this person, and then let them go. There are more advanced techniques for this, but there is no need to complicate things any more than you have to. Keep it simple.

- Clear out negative thoughts from your aura

The mental body is constantly interacting with other mental bodies, so you have the tendency to pick up negative thoughts that other people are thinking, along with your own. Negative thoughts have the ability to be fed for several years, especially if they are connected with any traumatic experience.

These types of thought-forms vibrate all through you in a way that causes a cascade reaction at every level of your energy: physical, etheric, emotional, mental, and spiritual. These energies cause you attract experiences, situations, and people into your life that has the same vibrational alignment. This means that if your energy is always negative, you will only attract negative experiences.

To help clear this pattern, take a look at your life and try to figure out you have been attracting things that you don't like. If you have been, then you are vibrating in alignment with these things. Some people refer to this as the law of attraction.

You need to start checking in with your energy field a few times a day, especially if you have been feeling off, to find out if you have created or picked up on any negative thought-forms and then consciously let them go.

When you do this, picture a white light cleaning your aura field from all debris and thought-forms that haven't been positively serving you.

- Balanced chakras

This was covered in an earlier chapter, but this is important to make sure you energy field stays clear. You can easily go through your

chakras twice a day to make sure your chakras stay cleared.

- Have a sacred space

You can create a sacred space anywhere in your home where you can spend the time with yourself, and where you can express yourself fully. This could be your office, a meditation room, or an art room. The only important thing is that this is only your room. This cannot be a shared space. It's fine if your pets and kids come in and out, that's hard to control, but they are just passing through. Your space also doesn't even have to be inside.

You can be as creative as you want, but this needs to be a place that you go to at least once a day. If you are unable to create an actual physical space, you can make one up in your mind and take the time to go there. You will be amazed at what your mind can come up with.

- Smudging

This is a must, and it's extremely effective. This should be done on a regular basis, especially if you have gone through a difficult situation. Use a bundle of white sage and smudge yourself and your house regularly.

- Connect with nature

Whenever you feel overwhelmed, take a nature walk, or a hike through the woods. Negative thoughts are typically only found in humans, so spending time in nature is a great way to recharge yourself. Connect with the landscape, water, flowers, and animals. And the great thing is, you can do it for free.

- Keep protective stones

These aren't because we need protection because we don't. Thinking you need protection will only cause negative emotions. Instead, these protective stones are a way to keep you grounded when you come in contact with negativity.

- Draw or journal

Expressing yourself is a great way to make yourself feel great. When you are feeling down, take some time to get creative. This could mean anything. Art is also a great form of natural healing.

- Sea salt bath

Sea salt does an amazing job at cleansing your energy. Sea salt can draw out negative energy. Whenever you are feeling energetically overwhelmed, take you a hot bath with some sea salt. The sea salt can be regular sea salt, Epsom salt, Himalayan salt, or any other kind you like.

Adding a few drops of essential oils to your bath is also a great idea. Make sure to test them first thought to make sure you don't have any allergies. Eucalyptus, citronella, and rosemary are the best ones to pick from.

Chapter 18: Positive Thoughts

The phrase positive thinking sounds great on the surface; most people would rather have positive thoughts rather than negative ones. But this phrase is also a fluffy term that is often easily dismissed within the real world. It doesn't carry the same kind of weight as a phrase like "hardworking" or "work ethic." But these kinds of views are changing.

People and research are telling us that positive thinking is not only about being happy, or pasting a smile on your face for the world to see. Positive thoughts add some real value to your everyday life and can help you to build skills that will last longer than a pasted on smile.

A positive psychology researcher from the University of North Caroline, Barbara Fredrickson, has helped to prove the power of positive thoughts on our everyday life. Let's look at some of what she has found, and what it means to you.

First, let's look at what negative thoughts will do to your brain. Imagine this for me.

Pretend you are walking along in the woods, and a tiger suddenly walks out on the path in front of you. When you see the tiger your brain will create a negative emotion, in this example, it would be fear.

Researchers, for a long time, have known that negative responses will cause you to perform a specific action. Like if a tiger crosses your path, you will likely run. Nothing else in the world, at that moment, matters. Your complete attention is on that tiger, the fear it has caused, and how you plan on getting away from it.

Basically, this means that a negative emotion will narrow the focus of your mind and thoughts. At the moment, you could have the choice to grab a stick, climb a tree, or pick up a leaf, but your brain will ignore these other options because they don't seem relevant when you have a tiger standing in front of you.

This is a great thing to have if you need to save life and limb, but in the world today, and in modern society, you don't have that fear of walking across a tiger in the woods. The bad thing is, the brain still has that programmed response to negative emotion, and it shuts out the rest of the world and limits what you see.

Another example will be if you are fighting with somebody. The emotions and anger you feel at that moment may completely consume you so much that you are unable to think about anything else. Or if you are stressing about all the things you need to do today, you might end up finding it hard to focus on the things you need to do or even to get started because the length of your to-do list has you paralyzed. Maybe you feel bad because you've not been eating healthy or exercising, and all you can think about is your willpower and thinking that you are lazy causing you not to have any motivation.

In all of these examples, your brain shuts you off to the outside world and focuses on the emotions of stress, fear, and anger, just like with the tiger. The only thing that negative emotion do is preventing your brain from seeing other options that may be around you. It's a survival instinct.

Now, what do positive thoughts do to the brain?

Fredrickson created an experiment to see the impact that positive emotions have on the brain. In the experiment, she split her subject into five separate groups and showed each of them a different movie clip.

Two of the groups were shown clips that cause positive emotions. One group was shown things that caused a sense of joy, and the second group was shown things that caused a sense of contentment.

The third group was the group the control group and they were only shown things that created no significant emotional change.

The other two groups were shown clips that would cause negative emotions. One of the groups saw images that caused fear, and the other was sown things that caused anger.

After they had seen the

images, all the participants were asked to picture themselves in a place that would cause that same emotion to come up and to write down the things that they would do. They were each handed a sheet of paper that had 20 fill-ins the blank lines that began with "I would like to…"

The participants that had been shown images that caused anger and fear weren't able to write down as many responses. While the participants that were shown images that caused contentment and joy were able to write many more actions than even the control group.

This means when you feel positive emotions such as love, joy, or contentment; you can see more things that you can do in life. This is some of the findings that showed that positive emotions could broaden your sense of possibilities and open up the mind.

But more interesting discoveries came later.

Benefits from positive emotions don't end when the emotion ends, in fact, you receive the most benefit from these emotions with an enhanced ability to build greater skills that you can use later in your life.

Look at this example. Children that run outside, swing along tree branches, and play with friends are developing physical, social, and creative skills by moving athletically, playing and communicating with others, and learning how to explore the world around them. This is because the emotions of joy and play are prompting the child to build these skill sets that will be valuable and useful to them later in life.

The skills that they have learned will last them a lot longer than the actual emotions that initiated the learning. Negative emotions have the opposite effect because building skills for the future are irrelevant to the brain at that moment in time when you have an immediate danger or threat.

As you can see these thoughts and emotions greatly impact your everyday life, so it's important that you learn more about positive self-talk and thinking.

Don't misunderstand what I mean by positive thinking either. This doesn't mean your turn a blind eye to the bad things in life. Positive thinking only means that you will approach these unpleasant moments productively and positively. You believe that only the best will happen.

Being able to think positively often starts with self-talk. If you don't know what self-talk is, it's the stream of unspoken communication that runs through your mind. These thoughts have the ability to be negative or positive. Self-talk can sometimes come from reason or logic, and it can sometimes arise from misconceptions because of the lack of information you have about something.

If your self-talk tends to be mainly negative, then your outlook on life is going to be mainly pessimistic. If your self-talk tends to be more positive, then you will be more optimistic.

Researchers, like Fredrickson, continue to explore all of the effects that optimism and positive thinking has on your health. A few of these benefits are:

- Better coping skills when you are facing stress or hardships
- Improved cardiovascular health and a reduced risk of dying from heart disease
- Improved physical and psychological well-being
- More resistance to the common cold
- Lower distress levels
- Lower depression rates
- A longer life

Negative self-talk normally comes in one of these four forms:

Polarizing

You tend to see things as either only good or only bad. You don't have a middle ground. You tend to feel as if you have to be perfect or you are a complete failure.

Catastrophizing

Your thoughts automatically go to the worst outcome possible. You regular coffee shop accidentally gets you order wrong, and you believe that the rest of your day is going to be horrible.

Third Eye Awakening

Personalizing

When something goes wrong, or something bad happens, you blame yourself for it. An example would be that you hear your friends night out was canceled, and you automatically think it's because nobody wanted to be around you, so they canceled.

Filtering

You increase the problems of the negative parts of a situation and completely ignore all of the positive ones. An example would be that you had an amazing day at work. You got everything done before you were supposed to, and your boss complimented you on your

speediness and quality of work. The evening, you only think about doing more tasks that next day and completely forget about the compliments you received from your boss.

Don't worry though; it's easy to change out your negative thoughts with positive ones, it will just take some time and effort. It's just like creating a new habit. Here are some ways to get started.

- Identify areas where you need to change

If you are looking to become more optimistic and practice more positive thinking, figure out the places and areas in your life where you tend to be more negative. This could be your commute to work, your relationship, anything. Start small by focusing only on one area at a time.

- Check yourself

Occasionally check in with yourself during the day to see what you're thinking. If you notice that your thoughts are mostly negative, try to figure out how you can turn them positive.

- Don't be afraid of humor

Allow yourself to laugh or smile, especially when you are going through something rough. Find the humor in everything that happens during the day. When you can laugh at life, then you will feel less stressed.

- Take up a healthy lifestyle

Try to exercise at least 30 minutes a few days a week. If you can't do 30 minutes at one time, your break it up into three ten-minute chunks. Exercise causes a positive effect on your mood and will help to reduce stress. Having a healthy diet will help to fuel your body and mind.

- Surround yourself with positivity

Make sure that the people you spend your time with and adds positivity to your life. They should be supportive and positive and can provide you with helpful feedback and advice. If you are surrounded by negative people, it will only increase your stress and your negativity.

- Practice positive self-talk

Follow this rule: don't say things to yourself that you would never say to your friend. You need to be encouraging and gentle. If negative thoughts come up, evaluate them with rational, and then say some positive affirmations. Think of the things that you are most thankful for.

Chapter 19: Energy Meditation

In this last section of meditations, you will find meditations that will help you gain more energy, and clear out your energy fields. These are perfect options for morning meditations so that you can set a positive tone for the rest of your day.

15 Minute Body Energy

Get into a comfortable position. This could seat with your legs crossed, or lie down in savasana. Close your eyes and take your focus to your body. Notice your breath, and simply notice the way that you breathe. In your mind's eye notice how you breath flows in and then flows out of your body. If you notice your attention beginning to wander around, gently bring it back to focus on your breathing.

When you inhale you are bringing life force, vitality, and energy into your body, and when you exhale you are releasing fatigue, negativity, and stress from your body. Allow these negative energies to drain out through your feet and disappear. Breathe in and breathe out. Continue to stay with deep, cleansing inhales and exhales, and take ten more.

Third Eye Awakening

With each of your inhales you are bringing in more energy to your body.

Feel this new subtle energy vibration spreading throughout your body all the way from your feet up to your head, and from your head down to your feet. Become aware of this tingling and warmth in every cell. Begin to visualize the positive energy that has begun to accumulate throughout your body and these energies shining as bright as the sun. Take this shining, glowing energy all the way to your crown at the top of your head. Take a deep breath in and release slowly. At the top of your head start to feel the warmth of this positive energy as it starts to radiate over your neck and face. Feel this new peacefulness and lightness in mind.

Take another deep breath in and slowly let it out. Notice the positive energy moving across your neck and shoulders, down both arms all the way to the fingertips, and across to your heart center. Feel this love and warmth feeling your heart. Let this positive healing energy to fill your body with unconditional love.

Take a deep cleansing breath. Now notice the healing energy moving down your body over your hips and down both legs to the tips of your toes. Notice how this energy helps to ground you to the earth. Feel supported, centered, and grounded. Take another cleansing breath. Your entire body is filled with this positive energy. Allow this energy to flow through your entire body freely. With every breath, you take to let this energy grow stronger. Take *three more deep, cleansing breaths.*

Focus your attention on your breathing and feel how this positive energy flows through your body. Take notice of this new sense of alertness and

clarity in your mind, vitality and energy in your body, and peacefulness and positivity in your soul. Let this positivity awaken your soul. Take a cleansing breath. Rest here with your breath and these feelings for the rest of your meditation, and take them with you throughout your day.

10 Minute Tranquility Meditation

Find a comfortable seated or lying position and close your eyes. Start to become aware of your breath. Notice the sensation of the breath as it enters through your nose with a cool sensation, and then as it warms as it travels gently into your lungs.

Fill up your lungs with a deep inhale, bringing in prana, energy, and vitality, your life force. While you exhale, feel how your body is releasing negativity, stress, and toxins that may have accumulated during your day.

Stay with your breath and focus on this feeling of deep inner peace for ten more inhales and exhales. Feel this positive energy that you have coursing through your body. Notice how every cell is tingling and warming.

Notice the energy that is in your surrounding environment, in all parts of nature, and in all living things. Take all of these energies and bring them together so that they feel as one. Picture these energies shining as bright as the sun.

Allow this ball of white shining energy into your crown at the top of your head. Then allow this white light to travel down your body. Notice how it is slowly warming your face and neck, and the traveling over your shoulders and down your arms and fingers. Notice as it moves across your chest, down your stomach, and over your hips, and then spreads down your legs, feet, and toes.

Your body is now filled with this warm, divine, white energy and light. Allow this healing light to fill every part of your body that needs to be healed. Feel all of its healing and warmth spreading throughout your surrounds.

Let this light bring you healing and peace to any emotional traumas or issues you may have. Shift your awareness to any desires or intentions that you may currently have. Hold onto these thoughts of your desires and intentions as you let this energy bring you your deepest wishes to life and your intentions to reality.

Feel how you are now connected to this divine light and energy, and remember that all is one. Stay with this new feeling of peacefulness, relaxation, and deepness for the remainder of your meditation.

Conclusion

Thank you for making it through to the end of this book. I hope it was informative and able to provide you with all of the knowledge and tools you need to achieve your goals and dreams, whatever they may be!

The next step is to start trying some of these techniques in your life and find out what works best for you.

Finally, if you found this book useful in any way, a review on Amazon is always appreciated! –Sarah Rowland!